Praise for *Beauty in the Breakdown*

"I admire greatly Julie's incredible talent and her exquisite beauty. She is a gracious and caring witness of how great and mighty God is, and her story is captivating!"

—BARBARA MANDRELL
COUNTRY MUSIC SUPERSTAR

"I met Julie Roberts back in about 2007. We both started out our careers around the same time, but she was soaring at heights I'd never reached. There was something about her that was just infectious, and I loved her voice and her humility so much.

"After many years had passed, I continued to think of her voice. When an opportunity and a song arose, I wanted to work with her in the studio and reached out to her. Soon, she became a close part of my family and my heart.

"She's an unbelievably kind soul and a fifty-pound story in a two-pound bag. Her struggles have inspired many and her triumphs even more. I'll believe in her 'til the day I die, and after reading this book, I guarantee all of you will as well. If you don't, you can come see me about it."

—SHOOTER JENNINGS
SINGER-SONGWRITER AND RECORD PRODUCER

"Julie is a star in every way. Her voice is beautifully strong, and she has a beautiful soul and appearance. Don't miss this!"

—JESSI COLTER
COUNTRY MUSIC ARTIST
AUTHOR OF *An O*

Beauty
in the
Breakdown

Beauty in the Breakdown

CHOOSING TO OVERCOME

Julie Roberts

with Ken Abraham

W PUBLISHING GROUP

AN IMPRINT OF THOMAS NELSON

Published in Nashville, Tennessee, by W Publishing, an imprint of Thomas Nelson.

Thomas Nelson titles may be purchased in bulk for educational, business, fund-raising, or sales promotional use. For information, please e-mail SpecialMarkets@ThomasNelson.com.

Any Internet addresses, phone numbers, or company or product information printed in this book are offered as a resource and are not intended in any way to be or to imply an endorsement by Thomas Nelson, nor does Thomas Nelson vouch for the existence, content, or services of these sites, phone numbers, companies, or products beyond the life of this book.

This is a work of nonfiction. The events and experiences detailed herein are all true and have been faithfully rendered as remembered by the author, to the best of her abilities. Some names and other identifying characteristics have been changed to protect the privacy of the individuals involved.

Unless otherwise noted, Scripture quotations are taken from the Holy Bible, New International Version®, NIV®. Copyright © 1973, 1978, 1984, 2011 by Biblica, Inc.™ Used by permission of Zondervan. All rights reserved worldwide. www.zondervan. com. The "NIV" and "New International Version" are trademarks registered in the United States Patent and Trademark Office by Biblica, Inc.™

Scripture quotations marked NASB are from New American Standard Bible® (NASB). Copyright © 1960, 1962, 1963, 1968, 1971, 1972, 1973, 1975, 1977, 1995 by The Lockman Foundation. Used by permission. www.Lockman.org

Quotation in chapter 18 taken from National Multiple Sclerosis Society, "What Causes MS?" https://www.nationalmssociety.org/What-is-MS/What-Causes-MS, accessed October 17, 2017.

ISBN 978-0-7852-1733-6 (eBook)

ISBN 978-0-7852-1959-0 (TP)

Library of Congress Cataloging-in-Publication Data
Library of Congress Control Number: 2018905107

Printed in the United States of America
18 19 20 21 22 LSC 10 9 8 7 6 5 4 3 2 1

To all the young girls in this world
who dare to dream big

I blame Mama for my love
of sad country songs.

Contents

Contents

1

From Dreams to Nightmares

Few people can truly say, "I am living my dream," but I really was. From my perspective, I had made it! Life was great. As a country music recording artist, I had achieved a gold album—a major milestone in the music world, signifying sales of more than five hundred thousand albums. I traveled on a beautiful tour bus, with a full band, singing concerts and meeting people all over the country. Mama joined me on the bus anytime she could break away from her full-time job as an accountant at a local mattress factory, and her presence made everything I was doing even more special to me.

I loved being on the road. I told my booking agent, "Keep me busy. The only time I want to come home is to work on my new album or to get my roots done." Of course, for me, the ultimate sign of my newfound success was that I was now a client of the same hairstylist who styled the hair of my childhood music idol, Barbara Mandrell! I know it seems silly, but that meant something significant to me. I was doing everything that I had envisioned and that I had asked God to allow me to do. My dreams of succeeding in the music business were coming true.

I was also working on my second album, hoping to follow the success of "Break Down Here," a hit song from my first album, *Julie Roberts*, and to keep the momentum going. I expected my career and my personal life to continue to flourish. Then, in a matter of seconds, my dreams turned to nightmares.

I was playing at the Orange Peel, a well-known club in Asheville, North Carolina, to an enthusiastic crowd pressed in tightly all the way to the front of the stage. More than one thousand people were packed into the venue, and the audience brimmed with enthusiasm. Many fans standing at the front of the stage knew my songs and sang the words along with me. It was a fabulous experience, something that most every music artist dreams of happening.

My band and I were putting on a great show, and everything seemed to be hitting just the right note—when suddenly, in the middle of my set, my vision became blurry and I lost the sense of feeling in my hands. Weird electricity-like shocks shot down my back from my head to my toes. Stark terror seared through me. *What's going on?* I thought. *This is weird!* The electric shocks dissipated quickly, and I didn't feel any other serious pain at the moment, but my eyesight remained blurred. I knew something was seriously wrong, but I kept on singing. I could hear people singing along with me, even though I could no longer see the audience members standing right in front of the stage.

I'm right-handed, so I was holding my microphone in that hand. When my hand went weak and then numb, I switched the mike to my left hand and continued the song. Then the same thing happened with my left hand. Now I was really scared. *I can't even hold on to the microphone!*

Fortunately, there was a microphone stand onstage, so I struggled awkwardly to place the mike on the stand and finished my full set standing almost motionless in front of it. As the band played a reprise of "Break Down Here," I walked toward the right side of the stage, where my tour manager met me and hooked his arm in mine, just as he did after each show. He aimed the beam of his flashlight on the floor so I could walk through the dimly lit backstage area. That night I needed his assistance more than ever.

Following the show, I wanted to sign pictures and albums for my fans, as I always did. *Whatever those strange sensations are in my body, I'll deal with them later,* I thought. I didn't want to disappoint the fans who were waiting patiently in line. I sat at a table and signed whatever anyone put in front of me, but I really couldn't see what I was writing. My sense of feeling in my fingers had returned slightly, so I could hold a Sharpie, but I was writing blindly. Fortunately, by that point in my young career, I had already signed a lot of autographs, so signing my name without seeing it wasn't that difficult.

After signing, I got back on the bus without saying a word about the unusual sensations and numbness to my road manager or to any of the guys in the band. Instead, I hurried straight to the back bedroom and called Mama. I explained about my vision being blurred and losing the feeling in my hands.

As soon as I told her what was going on, she said, "Julie, you need to come on home, just as fast as you can."

"I'm coming, Mama." I was really scared. I had never experienced anything like what had happened to me onstage that night. I knew something wasn't right.

Asheville is less than five hours from Nashville, so we were home before morning. Mama said, "You need to see a doctor." I made an appointment with my primary-care physician, who, upon hearing my symptoms, immediately sent me to a neurologist.

The neurologist recommended that I have an MRI. I had never had an MRI, and my first was a nightmare. For some reason, the doctor ordered an enclosed MRI for me. The attendant instructed me to lie down flat on a table, put a mask over my face, then slid me inside a tube. When the attendant put that mask on me, I became claustrophobic. My heart starting racing, and my whole body began perspiring profusely. All I could see was the mask covering my eyes, and that caused me to be even more fearful.

I had to hold completely still as the machine scanned my entire body, making all sorts of strange, loud clanking noises. *I gotta get out of this thing!* I screamed to myself. The MRI seemed to take forever, and I freaked out inside that cold tube. I felt as though I were in the scene in the movie *The Silence of the Lambs* where the girl is kept captive in the bottom of the well. I started kicking my feet, yelling, "Please let me out of here!"

The attendants came running at my first twitch, which, of course, meant that I had to redo the tests. The neurologist had also ordered a spinal tap, but before the hospital doctors could administer the test, I had to sign waivers and consent forms containing all sorts of ominous terminology and warnings. Although I had no idea what all was involved, I complied with the doctor's orders. I had never seen a needle that large in my life! I closed my eyes tightly and tried to think about something other than the pain.

After I completed the procedures, I was discharged from the hospital. The neurologist said, "I'll call you as soon as we know anything."

I went home and tried to forget about it, which was easy to do because I was feeling slightly better, and I had work to do on my new album.

I was in a studio in Franklin, Tennessee, about twenty miles south of Nashville, recording the song "Men and Mascara," with Byron Gallimore producing, when the doctor called me. I saw his name on my phone but didn't take the call because I didn't want to break the creative flow. I wanted to focus on the music, but I was anxious, wondering what news the doctor wanted to tell me. So I called Mama and asked her to get the results for me.

On my drive back to Nashville, I called Mama to learn the test results. I feared that the doctor had told her that I had a brain tumor. My palms were sweaty on the steering wheel. That was not like me.

When I got her on the phone, Mama quickly said, "Why don't you pull over, Julie, so I can talk to you?"

"No, I'm fine." I kept driving. "Just tell me, Mama. What did the doctor say?"

Mama listed a litany of things that I *didn't* have, things that apparently the doctor had told her the symptoms might have indicated, conditions that she had already looked up online.

"Okay, Mama." I was growing impatient. "That's fine. So tell me, what *do* I have?"

Mama seemed to take a deep breath before answering. "Well, the doctor says you have MS. They discovered some lesions on your brain."

"MS? Lesions on my brain? Wha . . . ?"

"Pull over," Mama said again. "I'm gonna come and pick you up."

"No, no. I can drive home," I said.

When I hung up, the first image that went through my mind was of Carol, a young woman in a nursing home where I used to sing many years earlier, who also had multiple sclerosis. Wheelchair-bound from an early age, her body debilitated, her life limited to the confines of that nursing home, I saw Carol.

And I saw me. I was twenty-six years old.

I knew now why I had met her. I knew my music had helped her overcome her daily despair. I was glad of that, but it scared me to think that my future might be similar to Carol's, confined to a wheelchair in a nursing home.

I had already overcome a number of difficult obstacles, but I had no idea how to face something like this. All I knew to do was to cry out to God for his help. I didn't ask him to heal me, although I believed that he could. My prayer focused more on how I was going to move forward with my life.

Tears welled in my eyes. "God, I don't know what you want me to do with my life," I prayed aloud. "Ever since I was a little girl, I've been convinced that the reason you put me on earth was to sing country music and to lift people's spirits. Now what?"

Of one thing I was certain: I wouldn't tell *anybody* outside my family that I had MS, not my best friends, not my record-label executives, not my band members—nobody. I suspected that if people on Music Row knew I had MS, they would regard me as "damaged goods." I had been in the music business long enough to know that it could be rather fickle—everybody wants you today, and tomorrow nobody knows your name. I especially worried that if the people at my record label or the concert promoters knew that I had this debilitating disease, they might assume that I couldn't perform up to par anymore and doubt that I could still sing and play shows.

I pulled into our driveway and saw Mama and my sister Lorie, who was now living with us, standing on the patio waiting for me, along with my dogs. Mama and Lorie were crying. Clearly, Mama had shared the bad news with my younger sister.

We hugged in the driveway and then went inside the house. "Why are y'all crying?" I asked them. I smiled at them, attempting to hide my own stress behind an everything-is-fine look, a skill that I had mastered early in life.

"Why aren't *you* crying?" Mama answered.

"I don't know," I said. "All I can think about is Carol. Maybe God wants me to do something else with my life. Maybe I'm supposed to help people like Carol, somehow."

I went to meet with the neurologist the following day. In a formal, clinical tone, he explained that multiple sclerosis is a disease that affects the brain, with residual ramifications throughout my body. "The exact causes of MS remain unknown," he told me, "but we have some hunches." He further explained that some people possibly get MS after having mononucleosis as a child. Females, especially, seem to contract MS at young ages. Others lack vitamin D, so doctors theorize that might have an impact.

I appreciated the doctor's information about my diagnosis but had already decided that I wasn't ready to accept it. The neurologist gave me lots of literature about MS and encouraged me to read it before we talked further about some sort of treatment protocol.

I'm sure it was important information, but it was overwhelming to me, and I was already zoning out, headed for my comfortable realm of denial. *Surely this isn't happening to me!* I thought.

I took the literature home and put it in a drawer, without reading a word of it. It was a coping strategy I had learned as a child: if I didn't talk about it, it didn't exist.

2

Escape!

"Hurry, girls," I heard Mama whisper hoarsely. "Come on. We have to get out of this house right now."

I had just celebrated my fifth birthday. My sister Lorie—a year younger—followed me as I crawled out of bed, both of us wearing our footie pajamas, rubbing the sleep from our eyes and wobbling precariously into the hallway leading from our bedroom to the living room. With my hair still in ponytails from the previous day, I grabbed my new Cabbage Patch doll and led Lorie toward the living room. Marie, our older sister by a few years, was already in the hall, carrying a blanket to keep us warm.

From Mama and Daddy's bedroom we heard a crash,

then frightening sounds of furniture scraping across the floor and Daddy rampaging through the room.

Mama glanced toward her and Daddy's bedroom door, right across the hallway from Lorie's and mine.

"Faster, girls. *Now!*" Mama whispered louder, clutching her nightgown around her neck. Her eyes looked red, her face swollen. "Get in the truck," she ordered. "Don't try to take anything else with you. Just go. Hurry!"

Mama shooed us out the front door, toward her white Ford F-150 pickup truck sitting at the edge of a row of shrubbery leading to the gray gravel driveway.

The cool night air slapped me wide-awake as Marie, Lorie, and I ran across the porch to the truck. Marie got there first. Mama always left the truck doors unlocked, so Marie jerked the door open, and the three of us piled inside. Mama followed closely behind, yelling back toward the door where, even in the dim light, we could see Daddy's tall, looming shadow.

Something must have clicked in Daddy's drunken brain, because he lurched out onto the porch and headed for the truck, just as Mama pushed the key in the ignition and turned it. The Ford roared to life, and Mama stretched her neck to the side so she could look over her shoulder to back out of the driveway.

"Get back inside this house!" Daddy yelled, staggering closer to us. "Where do you think you're going?"

Mama didn't answer, and she didn't stop; instead, she threw the pickup into reverse, the truck tires slinging gravel back in Daddy's direction.

I looked out the truck window, my face pressed against

the glass, terrified, as Daddy reached down and scooped up handfuls of gravel and hurled them at the truck.

Mama stopped the truck long enough to make sure we were okay. "Keep the windows rolled up," she instructed.

Daddy was so close now, he began kicking the front of the truck with his heavy work boot. Mama pressed down on the accelerator, and the truck roared backward. Daddy grabbed another handful of rocks and threw it at the windows. I reared back, instinctively. The stones crackled off the glass so loudly that I thought the window had shattered.

Mama kept going; she steered the truck backward down the gravel drive, finally hitting the pavement. She barely stopped for a fraction of a second before slamming the truck into drive, the tires peeling out on the road, heading toward Mawmaw and Pawpaw's house, while Daddy continued to rage at us from our front yard.

As soon as we had escaped to the highway, Mama leaned toward the dashboard and turned up the volume on the truck's stereo, filling the cab with country music.

"Let's sing, girls," she called above the loud music.

And we did. All three of us pajama-clad girls sang at the top of our lungs, pretending the incident we had just experienced—again, for the fourth time that month—had not even happened. Sadly, it would not be the last time Mama, my sisters, and I fled Daddy's erratic behavior.

Mama, Sandra Baker, married Daddy, Bobby Walton Roberts, in 1975 when she was twenty-five years old, knowing full well that he drank too much and smoked too much too. But he was tall, dark-haired, lean, handsome, and smart. Mama fell in love with him, and they eloped. Their first daughter, Marie, came along shortly after. Three years later, I was born, followed by our sister Lorie thirteen months later. My family settled in Mama's hometown of Lancaster, South Carolina.

Daddy was fabulously intelligent, worked as a nuclear engineer, and provided well for our family, even though we saw little of the money he earned. Daddy's money belonged to Daddy, not us. "It's my money," he often said, "and I will do what I want with it."

My sisters and I learned early on that if we needed something such as a winter coat or a new pair of shoes, we had to ask Daddy when he was drunk. Occasionally, when Daddy was the "good drunk," Mama could coax some money or a credit card out of him so we could go shopping. We had fun together on those shopping sprees, but Mama rarely bought anything for herself; she spent almost every extra penny she had on my sisters and me. Of course, when Daddy sobered up the next day and discovered what we had done, he would be furious. He would lash out at Mama, screaming at the top of his lungs.

Despite the tension between them, Mama worked hard trying to keep her husband happy. Mama ironed Daddy's clothes every week. If Mama didn't get the creases just right—or, more specifically—up to his impossibly unrealistic standards, then Daddy would lose his mind with frustration and anger, blistering Mama with profanity and other derogatory slurs. Maybe that's why I never learned to iron clothes well, nor did I ever learn to cook healthy meals, country-style food, or much of any-style food, for that matter, because I knew my best efforts would never meet Daddy's approval.

He was also moody, self-centered, and full of quirky contradictions. For instance, he complained about loud music even before he and Mama married. Yet Daddy loved music and played his own choices extremely loud—especially ZZ Top and other early 1970s and '80s rock-and-roll bands. He owned a huge stereo system, with speakers taller than my sisters and me, and when he cranked up the volume, the sound rattled the entire house.

We were never permitted to touch Daddy's stereo. One time, when Daddy was working, I played music on his stereo and turned it up so loud that it blew one of the tall speakers. He was furious when he discovered the broken speaker, but I didn't dare admit to breaking it.

He was also obsessive about his favorite hairbrush. If one of us girls used his brush and didn't put it back in the spot where he'd left it, Daddy pitched a fit. He would start yelling and wake up everyone in the house to help find his hairbrush. We usually discovered it near one of our dolls, where Marie, Lorie, or I had been brushing the doll's hair. When Daddy would leave, we'd use his hairbrush and turn up his stereo system really loud.

Daddy frequently retreated to the back of the house, just off the laundry room, to a small room he referred to as the "shop." "Don't go in the shop," he warned us frequently. His refusal to permit my sisters and me to enter that room only increased its mystery and intrigue in our young minds. Usually the door was closed, but one day when Daddy was out, Lorie and I noticed that the door to Daddy's man cave was open. We glanced around furtively, then ducked inside the forbidden room. There was a computer on a desk, and off to the side were Daddy's weights that he used to work out. We snooped around like two commandos, exploring every nook and cranny, careful not to move or disturb anything. Surprisingly, there was nothing all that special about the area, except that Daddy kept his prized items there, including a stash of dirty magazines that we found. When we showed the explicit materials to Mama, she didn't seem surprised.

We had to whisper when Daddy was in the house, and especially when he was asleep or hungover from his binge drinking the previous night. He'd go to bed early because he got up early, so we had to play our music quietly. He would scream at my sisters and me whenever our music was even moderately turned up. Looking back now, I recognize that Daddy was a functioning alcoholic. People who didn't know him well might never have imagined that he had a problem. He was disciplined enough to get up early every morning, run six miles, and shower before driving to work in Charlotte, where he performed his duties well as a nuclear engineer. But then he would stop at the liquor store on the way home and drink a pint of scotch before he pulled in our driveway. Thankfully, he never had a car accident while driving, and he never got stopped by the police for a DUI, although maybe that would have been a blessing. He drank all the way home and then continued drinking after he got home.

Nobody in our family openly admitted that Daddy was an alcoholic. It was as though if we didn't talk about the situation, it wasn't happening. If we didn't say it out loud, it wasn't real. Choosing not to talk about difficult things was a coping mechanism that I learned to use in numerous other areas of my life, and it did not serve me well.

Because of my father's alcoholism and abusive behavior, I never invited any of my friends to our home—especially for overnight stays, which are always popular with teenage girls. We didn't dare do that because we never knew what Daddy's condition and attitude might be. Which Daddy would show up when he came home: good Daddy or mean Daddy? Sober Daddy or drunk Daddy? Besides, Daddy went to bed early, and we had to be quiet so he could sleep. That wouldn't work well for sleepovers with a bunch of giggling girls.

When Daddy went out of town, Mama and we girls breathed a little easier. We could let down our hair and laugh, play music as loudly as we wanted, and have fun without the fear of disturbing Daddy.

Daddy was also a clean-freak. He placed a plastic runner over the carpet in the hallway of our house to help keep the carpet clean. On those nights when Daddy drank too much, the squeaking sound of his shoes on that plastic runner was an ominous warning sign for us. That, and the sound of Daddy's shoulders rubbing against the wall as he staggered down the hallway, alerted us that it might be time to run for Mama's pickup truck again.

Sometimes Daddy was downright dangerous when he drank too much. He never hit me, although he screamed at all of us—a lot. But he did hit my older sister, Marie.

On one occasion, Marie and I foolishly wrote on the wall with crayons. When Daddy came home and saw it, he took his belt and beat Marie, screaming at her the entire time. I cowered in fear in our bedroom.

When Mama found out, she threatened Daddy. "If you ever do that again, I will kill you!" And I honestly think she would have.

Daddy did not respond well to Mama's threat. Although I never saw my father physically strike my mother, Mama often went to work with black eyes, bruises, scrapes, and other marks on her body that I'm sure were a result of some of her fights with Daddy. She wore long sleeves to hide the marks on her arms. I never heard any of Mama's coworkers talk about it, but I'm sure they knew.

I once overheard Mama tell Daddy, referring to her bruises, "The next time you do that when you come home drunk, I'm going to drop a sheet over your head and beat you with a frying pan!"

At the time I didn't think Mama was serious, but she might have been.

I didn't know what a normal family looked like; I'd never seen normal. I didn't really know what "normal" was.

Mawmaw and Pawpaw, my maternal grandparents, lived only five miles away from us. Regardless of the time of day or night, or the reason for our unexpected visits, Mawmaw always welcomed us. Besides loving us, she could relate to Mama's predicament because, long before I was born, Pawpaw had also been hard to live with. Even now, he was rarely home when we showed up. He owned a convenience store and often drank himself to sleep there, staying at the store all night. In addition to managing the store, his variety of jobs included driving a yellow taxi. By the time I came along, Pawpaw had mellowed, and I remember him as a kind, although absent, man. Mama warned me, though, that when it comes to men, things aren't always as they seem.

One reason that Daddy didn't follow us on the nights we went to our grandparents' house was because he was afraid of Pawpaw's response. He knew that Pawpaw would come out with a shotgun and force him to leave.

Whenever we stayed with Mawmaw and Pawpaw, Daddy would call Mawmaw's phone incessantly, wanting to speak to Mama, but she wouldn't take his calls. Mawmaw would serve as the call screener. "Bob, she doesn't want to talk to you right now," Mawmaw would tell him. Other times, Daddy might send flowers to Mama at her workplace to convince her that he was sorry, and we'd usually go back home that night.

Going to Mawmaw and Pawpaw's house was our escape, and once we got there, I didn't want to return home. During my early childhood, we spent more nights at Mawmaw's than we did in our own beds. That was okay with me; I didn't want to go back to "Daddy's house."

Of course, it was our house, too, but Daddy never allowed us to feel that it was Mama's and our home. He gave the impression that he *permitted* us to live there, since he was the one who earned the money to pay the bills.

The truth is, Mama worked as hard as Daddy. She had a background in accounting and held several different jobs during my childhood. Daddy's salary paid the house payment, but Mama covered all our household expenses out of her own paycheck.

As one of her jobs, Mama managed the Carriage Inn, a local motel in town. That was a fun place for my sisters and me to play while Mama was working. If we were sick and absent from school, Mama took us to work with her and allowed us to stay in one of the motel rooms, where we'd watch television all day. We could laugh and play music as loudly as we wanted, and Mama let us order club sandwiches, french fries, and sweet tea from the motel restaurant.

But the motel also had a bar where Daddy went to drink, and when he drank, he often danced with the waitresses and other women at the motel bar. On several occasions, my sisters and I went to the motel with Mama and witnessed Daddy's flirtatious behavior. Although we couldn't prove it, we assumed that he was being unfaithful to Mama.

Things calmed down for a brief season when Daddy moved his mom into our house. Granny Lambert had Parkinson's disease. Her mind worked well, but her body would not function correctly. Nevertheless, I loved Granny Lambert, and to my eight-year-old spirit, she was a soothing balm in the midst of the chaos and pain in our home.

Granny Lambert was strong in her Christian faith, and she was not afraid to speak up about what was right and wrong. One day when Granny heard Daddy cussing and railing at Mama about the ironing, she interrupted him. "Just stop," she said firmly. "That's enough."

Amazingly, Daddy calmed down. For the next eight months, as long as Granny Lambert lived with us, Daddy remained sober and less abusive; but as Granny's health declined, he drank more to cope with her dying. The only time I saw Daddy cry was at Granny Lambert's funeral. His face was puffy, and he wore dark glasses most of the time we were there.

Daddy was okay for a while, and then his behavior relapsed back to "drunk Daddy." He played Elton John's song "Candle in the Wind" over and over again as he drank himself into a nightly stupor. He didn't cry, but I could tell he was sad. Before long, he reverted to his previous violent patterns.

Eventually, I said, "Mama, let's leave and go to Mawmaw's and stay there. We don't have to live like this."

Mama looked at me with a hint of a smile, as though considering my suggestion. I didn't realize that Mama was already planning her escape.

Years later, when I was an adult, Mama told me that because of Daddy's suspected infidelity, his alcoholism, and abusive behavior, she had considered divorce, but Mawmaw had advised against it. "This is a small town and people talk," Mawmaw said. "Divorce would be hard on the girls at school. Stay with him till the girls are grown up."

That made sense to Mama, so she resigned herself to living with an abusive husband. She told me that even as she rocked Lorie as a baby, she was already dreaming of the day when she could escape Daddy's abuse and negative influence.

"I'll stay till you are eighteen," Mama said she would whisper to baby Lorie, "and after that, I'm getting out." Assuming, of course, that she and Daddy didn't kill each other in the meantime.

Mama was our protector. She never left us alone at home for fear of what might happen if Daddy had been drinking. Even if it meant inconvenience and sacrifice for her, she'd drag us out of bed in the middle of the night when Daddy was belligerent and tearing up the house, and she'd drive us to Mawmaw's house so we could get a quiet night's sleep for school. She endured the pain and embarrassment of walking around with those black eyes and bruises so her girls wouldn't get touched by the man she married—the man we called Daddy.

Consequently, my childhood was a convoluted mishmash of emotions. I was quiet and scared, nosy and inquisitive; a blonde-haired, blue-eyed, sweet child. I was a dreamer and a pleaser; I wanted everyone to be happy.

At the same time, I was afraid of many things. I was scared of people in general, and I didn't trust anyone—especially men. I thought every man was like Daddy. I didn't know what it meant to have a kind, considerate man in my life, someone who loved me unconditionally.

Most of all, I was scared to be in my own home with my dad. And I was scared Daddy was going to hurt the most important person in my life—Mama. I feared Daddy would get drunk enough that he'd kill Mama one day.

The domestic violence intensified when Daddy came home from the motel one night in an amorous mood. That probably would have been okay, had he not been drinking, dancing, and flirting with other women. Apparently, when he flopped into bed and pressed Mama for sexual intimacy, she wanted nothing to do with him. He kicked her so hard in her back that she flew all the way out of the bed and landed on the floor.

Feisty even while in pain—perhaps more so—Mama got to her feet and the fight was on, moving out of the bedroom, into the hall, and then into the living room. At first Lorie and I pulled the covers over our heads and cowered in fear, but as the yelling and vitriol increased, I knew I had to do something.

Although I was only eleven years old, from somewhere in my soul, I found the courage to start protecting this amazing woman. I ran out into the living room and saw Mama and Daddy faced off in front of each other. I stepped in between them just as Daddy raised his arm as though he was going to strike Mama.

I yelled, "Leave her alone, Daddy! Don't touch her. If you're gonna hit someone, you're gonna have to hit me this time!"

The room fell suddenly silent. Daddy stood glaring at me, his open palm still raised as though he was going to slap me across the face. But he didn't. Instead, he slowly lowered his arm to his side, and both Mama and I stepped around him and out of the room.

Mama gathered my sisters, and we left, singing all the way to Mawmaw's. Along the way, I told Mama, "Don't let him see you cry." I didn't want Daddy to know that he had that sort of power over her.

"I'm trying," she said, "but it is hard. He's just so mean."

"It won't be this way forever, Mama," I said. "Don't let him think we are weak."

For many years, that was my guiding principle. No matter what Daddy did, I refused to let him see tears in my eyes.

3

God, Make Me a Singer Like Barbara Mandrell

Mama did all she could to keep our childhood normal, and saying my prayers with her every single night was the one constant I could count on. Although I memorized my prayer and said it the same way every time, Mama always seemed eager to sit by my bed and listen intently as I prayed. I meant every word, too, from the bottom of my young heart:

"Now I lay me down to sleep; I pray the Lord my soul to keep. If I should die before I wake, I pray the Lord my soul to take. God bless Mama, Daddy, Marie, Lorie, Mawmaw, Pawpaw, Aunt Rhonda, Aunt Crystal, Spike [our dog], and Gray Ball [our cat]. God, please help Mama to stop smoking and Daddy to quit drinking. And God, please give me a record deal and Mama a happy home. Amen."

I wasn't quite sure what a record deal involved, but I asked God for one every night. I loved country music, especially the sad country songs we listened to during our middle-of-the night drives in Mama's white truck. She'd turn the music up, and we'd sing songs by Dolly Parton, Waylon Jennings, Elvis, and Patsy Cline. Those car rides in the middle of night actually became fun, and strangely, I felt safe and secure, even though we were running for our lives. To this day, when I hear one of those songs, I'll say, "That's a 'white truck' song."

My country-music role model was Barbara Mandrell. As a little girl, I watched Barbara and her sisters on television in their NBC-TV hit show, *Barbara Mandrell and the Mandrell Sisters*. The show followed Barbara's country radio hit, "I Was Country When Country Wasn't Cool," which, along with sold-out concerts, helped garner for Barbara the Country Music Association's Entertainer of the Year Award in 1980 and again in 1981.

Her sisters, Irlene and Louise, were gorgeous, but Barbara especially caught my attention. A petite blonde with sparkling eyes, she looked and sounded fantastic. She sang, danced, and played all sorts of instruments, and I loved her. I wanted to look like Barbara, dance like Barbara, and sound like Barbara. I wanted to *be* Barbara Mandrell!

Although I didn't realize it, during all those dashes to our grandparents' house, Mama was listening to me sing. She recognized that I was singing on pitch and in key. Mama was a great singer herself, and she played piano. Even though she knew how to read music, she played all the old hymns by ear.

When I was only six years old, Mama signed me up for private voice lessons from Ms. Holford, a highly regarded teacher who lived in Camden, South Carolina, about a thirty-minute drive from Lancaster. A tall, confident brunette, Ms. Holford helped me not only with my voice but also my stage gestures, poise, posture, and the art of performing. "Hold your hand like this as you sing," she advised. "Stand straight. Enunciate!"

Ms. Holford stressed the importance of warming up. "Your voice is your instrument for life," she said, "so you have to protect it. That's why it's important to do vocal warmups before singing." She took her music seriously and expected me to practice her recommendations and have my performances down pat. Mama sat in the room with me during my voice lessons because I was nervous and didn't want to disappoint Ms. Holford. Nevertheless, after a few lessons, Ms. Holford and Mama felt I was ready for my first talent competition. I planned to sing "Rocky Top," a song first popularized by the Osborne Brothers and then later made a hit by country artist Lynn Anderson in the early 1970s. By the time I heard the song, it had already become a standard.

Mawmaw had sewn a special white one-piece outfit made from satiny material and decked out with rhinestones for me to wear as I performed in public for the first time. With all the sparkle, when I nervously stepped to the center of the stage, I literally shined!

The only movement I made during the song was to tap

my right foot, something I still do to this day when I perform. At the end, I slowly lifted my hand in classic showbiz style, just like Mama and Ms. Holford had taught me.

My performance, however, lacked luster. I realized two things from my singing debut that night—two lessons that I still take with me. One, never eat greasy fried okra or squash before singing, because you might burp in the middle of your performance. Yep, you guessed it. That's what I had eaten for dinner, and what can I say? I burped during the first verse!

More positively, the second lesson I discovered was that I felt safe onstage. No one could hurt me up there—the audience was kind to the competitors, regardless—and, because there were so many competitions in our area, if I kept doing them, we could be gone from home every Saturday night and, more importantly, away from Daddy. That made the momentary anxiety I experienced before performing worthwhile.

Following my dubious debut, Mama entered me in a number of children's pageants. Mama sold Avon products and used her earnings to pay for my music lessons and the contest entry fees. Mawmaw made many of my dresses and singing outfits. Occasionally, Mama bought me a new dress at our town's most popular dress store, the Diane Shop, which specialized in children's pageant wear. Anna Sue Love, the store owner, allowed Mama to make payments on the dresses and even permitted her to bring the dresses back for resale after I had worn them a few times.

The only beauty contest that I ever won was Little Miss Lancaster, a prestigious event because it was connected to the Miss South Carolina pageant. I placed high in plenty of others and took home a bunch of trophies and crowns. I didn't really like the beauty pageants, but I did enjoy the talent competitions, so Mama found more talent contests in which I could sing. Many events were conducted by local Rotary or Kiwanis Clubs, Shriners organizations, and other civic groups. Most had small cash prizes, trophies, or crowns.

Mama liked "Break It to Me Gently," a song by Juice Newton, and she wanted me to sing it. A tearjerker, it wasn't exactly the type of song that a preadolescent girl usually would sing at a pageant, but since it meant something to Mama, I learned it. The audiences at the competitions loved hearing a little girl sing such a grown-up song, and I won a lot of talent contests!

The applications for the contests contained questions such as, "What is your favorite television show?" and "What is your favorite food?"

At the time, the only TV show I could name other than the Mandrells' was *The Carol Burnett Show*, which I enjoyed watching at Mawmaw's house because it made Mama laugh, even though I didn't understand many of the jokes and gags. I also watched *Hee Haw* with my sisters, and we thought that show was hilarious. Favorite food? That was easy. Anything sweet or fried!

The pageants also asked grandiose questions such as, "What is your ambition in life?"

Ambition? I didn't even know what the word meant, but

I replied, "I want to be a singer like Barbara Mandrell." The judges loved it!

Ms. Holford kept Mama informed about upcoming events throughout the county. I competed in dozens of contests and soon discovered that junior beauty pageants were not for me. Besides the entry fees and costs for photographs, contestants were expected to secure ads from local papers. Many of the girls competing seemed to come from wealthy families. Their costumes looked as though they had stepped right out of a fashion magazine. Mine were from patterns homemade by Mawmaw. She was a great seamstress, and we appreciated the love she poured into each outfit, but it was difficult to compete with the lavish costumes the more affluent kids wore.

Even so, I knew even as a little girl that I wanted to keep singing in public. I loved singing, and I loved being "on the road," even if it meant traveling only to a neighboring county. Mama, my sisters, and I had the most fun on the road. We couldn't afford to eat at restaurants, so we limited our expenses by packing picnic foods in coolers. Mawmaw brought the fried chicken and deviled eggs. We'd pull in at a rest stop along the road and enjoy our meal. I'd say, "Someday we're going to be on a big bus doing this!"

Daddy never asked how I fared at the pageants and talent contests, whether I'd won or lost. He didn't seem to care. I longed for him to come hear me sing, but he never seemed interested. He never said, "I believe in you," or anything that might bolster my confidence.

On only one occasion did Daddy suggest a song for me to sing. "You should do Hank Williams's song, 'I'm So Lonesome

I Could Cry,'" Daddy said flatly. I listened to the song, and I could identify with the lyrics. So I learned to sing it. Years later, on the one occasion when Daddy came to hear me sing, I performed "I'm So Lonesome I Could Cry" onstage. Daddy never said a word about it.

Yet for some strange reason, despite his meanness, as a little girl, I craved even the slightest indication of approval I received from Daddy. Not that he waited up to welcome us. When we got home, we'd find him slumped in his chair, staring blankly at the television. He'd grunt as we came in, and I'd hurriedly go to my bedroom to change clothes before he noticed that I was wearing my show clothes.

Mama was my cheerleader. She loved for me to sing "Rocky Top," and when I sang it at school, my teachers enjoyed it too. But my classmates laughed and mocked me for singing "hillbilly music." They were more into artists such as Debbie Gibson, Tiffany, and other pop artists. When my classmates would see me walking down the hall at school, they'd start sniggering and singing "Rocky Top" in mocking voices. As they passed me, they'd break out laughing. I was embarrassed and felt self-conscious. Often, when I saw my classmates coming toward me, I'd lower my eyes and hope they wouldn't notice me. But they rarely let me get away so easily. Although we lived in Lancaster, South Carolina, where country music played every day on the radio, in grocery stores, and in most people's cars, it wasn't considered cool for a kid to sing country music.

Despite the schoolkids' teasing, I complied with Mama's wishes that I sing "Rocky Top." Eventually, though, I admitted my frustrations to her. "Mama, I love to sing, but I don't want to sing *that* song in school anymore because everyone makes fun of me every time I sing it."

"They're just jealous," Mama responded. "Remember what Barbara Mandrell said in 'I Was Country When Country Wasn't Cool' about her listening to the Opry while all her friends were listening to rock and roll. You keep doing what you love, and it will all work out."

The kids at school weren't the only ones to make fun of me. Daddy did too.

Daddy was obsessed with his own physical fitness. Despite his heavy drinking, he exercised every day and kept his weight under control. Maybe because his body was sleek and slender, he was quick to notice that the other members in our family were not. My sisters and I were a bit pudgy and overweight, so Daddy called us "the three little pigs." That didn't do much for our self-images.

Mama worked hard, but she didn't spend her money on herself. She spent her money on us girls, and especially on background soundtracks so I could sing with musical accompaniment. She often put off buying basic staples if I needed a new soundtrack. "We don't need to buy toilet paper this week," she quipped. "We'll use that money for music tracks."

She also bought me an inexpensive microphone and a boom box so I could practice singing to the tracks, since I couldn't yet play an instrument. I set up my little boom box in the living room and pressed Play. But I didn't get far into the song.

"Get outside with all that noise!" Daddy yelled.

Although Daddy enjoyed music, he didn't enjoy mine. He would not tolerate me practicing my music in the house, so, on hot days or cold, he forced me to go outside on the front porch or into the garage to sing to my soundtracks. That was discouraging because I wanted to make Daddy as proud of me as Mama was. To overcome my disappointment, I pretended the front porch was my stage. I sang as loudly as I could toward the imaginary audience in the front yard. Although Daddy didn't hear me sing, the neighbors sure did!

Often, Mama joined me in the garage, surrounded by several stray cats that I had been caring for—I almost always had a couple of animals because I took in every stray dog or cat that came my way, and they all seemed to multiply. Standing next to Daddy's motorcycle, various car parts, and all his stuff in the heat of summer or the chill of winter, I'd practice singing in the garage, without air-conditioning or heat.

One day while I was singing in the garage, Mama sat in a folding chair, smoking cigarettes while I practiced. Between puffs, she offered her advice. "Hold that note a little longer on that part," she said. "On that word, point directly at the audience while you sing it," she instructed. She was a stage mom long before I ever played a big-time arena.

Suddenly, the door leading to the house opened, and Daddy stuck out his head. "Hey, Sandra," he yelled angrily at Mama. "Keep it down out here!" He slammed the door and went back inside.

Mama looked at me, then turned her head away so she could curse Daddy under her breath without me seeing or hearing her. But I knew.

"Okay, let's try that part again," Mama said.

Maybe because I loved Barbara Mandrell and the Mandrell Sisters, Mama got the idea that "the Roberts Sisters" could perform together. Mawmaw made different colored, perfectly fitted jumpsuits for each of us, and we looked sharp. We sang songs such as "Anything You Can Do (I Can Do Better)" and other show tunes. Marie, Lorie, and I sang at all sorts of local programs and pageants, sponsored by various civic groups around Lancaster. The same woman, Susan Connelly—"Miss Susan," as we called her—ran all the pageants. Ms. Connelly owned a dance studio, so she was constantly on the lookout for new talent.

Mama enrolled my sisters and me in Ms. Connelly's dance classes, where we learned tap, jazz, and ballet. Mama saved enough money to buy us dance shoes and outfits, and we participated in all the dance recitals. Lorie and I were terrible. We didn't memorize the dances or even like to practice, so we did our best to stay in the back lines during recitals so nobody would notice us. I enjoyed dancing, but I wasn't good at it. Marie, on the other hand, excelled. She took to dancing like I took to singing, and a few years later, Ms. Connelly hired Marie as an instructor.

It's amazing the positive influence that a teacher can have, even on someone surrounded by negative influences. In my junior high school, being in the chorus was considered cool. Even the athletes wanted to participate, and I did too.

My junior high chorus teacher, Jay Forrest, saw potential in me. He assigned solos to me that were envied by all the other kids in chorus. I sang songs such as the Crosby, Stills, Nash & Young hit "Teach Your Children," and at Christmas, Mr. Forrest arranged a hip, contemporary version of "White Christmas" for me to sing.

"Go for it, Julie," he encouraged me. "Don't hold back."

Mr. Forrest's encouragement was a pivotal point not only in my singing but also in my gaining acceptance with my peers. They stopped making fun of me. Suddenly, I was no longer the hillbilly singing "Rocky Top," but I was the voice everyone wanted to hear. Mr. Forrest continued to teach me vocal techniques, and, more importantly, he helped me to step out of my comfort zone and find a confidence I hadn't had previously in front of my peers. With Mr. Forrest's reassurance, I overcame my fear of being teased.

Mama and her youngest sister, my aunt Crystal, regularly booked me at various festivals all over South Carolina and northern Georgia. In the local library, Mama and Crystal found directories listing special events scheduled in the Carolinas. As my first booking agents, they pitched me to every festival possible. I sang at apple festivals; peach festivals; the Flopeye Fish Festival in Great Falls, South Carolina;

and all sorts of other events. I became popular in school and was making good grades, but I still was not really well known, since I was gone every weekend singing somewhere. My classmates had no idea of my stage persona!

Three years ahead of me in school, Marie was no longer interested in the festival circuit. She focused more on academics, her social life, and her dancing. Lorie came to my performances along with Mama and Aunt Crystal, but she didn't care to sing anymore, so it was just me up there onstage.

And I loved it! I sang one song after another during my thirty-minute slots at festivals. I almost always sang "No One Needs to Know" by Shania Twain, and I usually ended my set with "Break It to Me Gently." I didn't yet have a lot of life experience to draw upon for between-song banter, so I mostly stuck to introducing the songs and singing my heart out.

Mama always wanted me to do Martina McBride's hit "Independence Day," a song about a woman leaving her man, but Martina sang in a much higher range than I did.

"I can't do that song, Mama," I protested. "I can't sing as high as Martina."

"Yes, you can!" she said. "Saang it!" Mama believed in me more than I believed in myself. Much to her chagrin, I never did sing Martina's song, even though I knew Mama regarded it as a hopeful anthem.

I took a few piano lessons and performed several recitals, but I got bored quickly with the traditional formal music lessons, learning scales and theory. I wanted to play! And I really wanted to learn how to play a guitar. Mama found Don Hargett, a guitar teacher in Monroe, North Carolina, about a forty-five-minute drive away from us. He worked with children and was reasonably priced at fifteen dollars for a thirty-minute lesson.

My first guitar came from a yard sale. Aunt Crystal and Uncle Philip bought it for me for twenty-five dollars. It didn't have a case, so I just carried it with me. Every week, my guitar teacher tuned it before my lesson because I did not know how to tune the guitar myself.

Rather than teaching with a traditional approach, in which I'd learn all sorts of drills, scales, and music theory, Mr. Hargett won my heart when he asked, "Julie, what song do *you* want to learn to play?"

I didn't really know.

"How about this?" He played "Should've Been a Cowboy" by Toby Keith. I recognized the song from hearing it on the radio. "Do you like that song?" Mr. Hargett asked.

I lit up. "Yeah, I love that song," I said.

That was the first song I learned to play on my inexpensive guitar.

Mr. Hargett gave lessons in his recording studio, so I took my soundtracks, and he transposed some of them to a better key for my voice, usually lower than the original. I patterned my style after Tanya Tucker, whom I regarded as an original, so he helped me learn to play some Tanya Tucker songs, and of course, some Barbara Mandrell material too.

Several years later, when Daddy saw that I was serious about learning to play, he bought me a round-backed

Ovation guitar for Christmas. He even picked it out himself. It was his one contribution to my music career. He never came to hear me play it, but he purchased it for me, and I appreciated the gift.

In addition to teaching me how to play the guitar, Mr. Hargett also taught me the Nashville number system, used in most studios in Music City. Unlike note-filled sheet music, the number system is based on chords, with each chord assigned a number, allowing room for a lot of improvisational musicianship. Even highly skilled professional musicians use the Nashville number system in the studio or when running down an arrangement.

Mr. Hargett also taught me how to use a miracle-working little device known as a capo, a sort of rubber-covered bar that clamped on my guitar strings and allowed me to raise the pitch of the strings, changing the key, but I could still use the same fingering patterns. Wow! That opened a whole new world of music to me.

At one of the many festivals where I sang, Mama and I met a woman named Pat Coates, the marketing director for WHRM-FM, one of our local radio stations. She loved country music and invited me to sing at various promotions and charity benefits sponsored by her station.

Pat's brothers, Bill and Oscar Coates, had a band that played around our area. On the first Saturday of every month, they went to a couple of nursing homes to play for the residents and staff.

After hearing me sing, Pat approached Mama and me and told us about her brothers. "You should sit in with them sometime when they sing at the nursing homes," she told me. "The residents would absolutely love you."

I was only twelve years old, pushing thirteen. All the members of the band were in their sixties or seventies. Besides Oscar and Bill, they had a preacher who played steel guitar and a man nicknamed Blackie who played bass. Compared to me, those guys seemed really old! But they allowed me to sit in with them at the nursing homes, and I discovered that they were good musicians. I enjoyed singing with them.

We performed familiar gospel songs, such as "Peace in the Valley," "Precious Memories," and "I'll Fly Away," as well as a few country music favorites. Our lead vocalist, Oscar, sang with such a bluesy feel to his voice, people couldn't help listening to him. Similar to Patsy Cline, Oscar could take a lyric and *own* it.

Sometimes in the middle of a song, I'd find myself staring at Oscar in admiration, wondering, *How does he put that kind of emotion into a song?* I credit Oscar with not only modeling that bluesy style but also inspiring me to sing with a similar sort of soul. I have always sung in a slightly lower register than many other female artists, and rather than trying to change that, Oscar encouraged me to develop a soulful sound in my voice. More than anyone in my career, Oscar influenced my vocal style.

Each month, we returned to play at the same two nursing homes, a state-run convalescent center and a privately run home known as White Oak Manor, both in Lancaster.

At White Oak Manor, I noticed a younger woman smiling at me from a wheelchair. I found out that her name was Carol, and she was "thirty-several" years of age.

Carol didn't look like many of the other people in the nursing home, some of whom had Alzheimer's disease or other forms of dementia, or had suffered from a stroke or other debilitating diseases. She dressed stylishly and wore attractive makeup. I noticed Carol always wore bright-red lipstick.

She asked me to sing "Peace in the Valley" and Lorrie Morgan's song "What Part of No," which I was glad to do. Carol tried to clap but couldn't quite get her hands to function correctly. I was happy to bring some small pleasure to Carol, but I was also concerned for her. I wondered, *What is she doing here?*

"Mama, why is Carol so young and living in the nursing home?" I asked.

Mama asked around among the staff, and somebody told us that Carol had MS. "Multiple sclerosis," the aide explained, "is a disease that affects the body's motor system." Carol did not have a caretaker in her own home, so she lived at the nursing home.

At the time, I knew very little about MS. All I knew was that country music made Carol smile, and although I couldn't figure it all out, I felt that God had allowed me to meet Carol for a reason.

4

There Is No Plan B

I was popular in school and made straight As—until I encountered a teacher I could never please. This was devastating not only because I desperately wanted everyone to like me but also because she taught chorus, a class in which I had every reason to believe I'd do well. But no matter how hard I worked, she withheld her approval.

Ultimately, I ended up with a B in her class—my first B ever—but I learned a lesson far more important than the grade: even if I gave my best, there would be adversities over which I had little control. I decided that I wouldn't let that keep me from my dreams. In fact, that experience made me even more determined.

I adored Trisha Yearwood's singing, so while I was still

in high school, Mama gave me the book *Get Hot or Go Home*, a biography about Trisha Yearwood's early life and career. Fascinated by how Trisha's music career developed, I noticed that she had attended Belmont University in Nashville, a relatively small Christian college located within walking distance of Music Row, the nickname given to Sixteenth to Eighteenth Avenues, where many famous recording studios and music companies are located.

Reading Trisha's story planted the seed in my heart and mind to attend Belmont, even though I knew little about the college and had never even visited the campus. I did some research and discovered that Belmont offered a degree in music business. That appealed to me, and Mama was okay with it, as long as I earned a degree. I was discouraged to learn that Belmont's tuition, room, and board didn't fit into my meager budget, but I knew I wanted to get to Nashville eventually. I already saw myself attending Belmont, so during my high school years, my guidance counselor helped me select courses that would be accepted by Belmont.

I had started working as soon as I was old enough to get a job, first at a grocery store and then at a snow cone shop. During the summer of my senior year of high school, I sang in a country music revue at Carowinds, a nearly four-hundred-acre amusement and water park on the border of North and South Carolina, near Charlotte. I wanted to save money for college, but I also secretly wanted to earn enough money to rescue Mama from the abusive relationship in which she lived.

I plotted, planned, and prayed for my mother's escape. For sure, part of my goal of becoming a country music star stemmed from my desire to buy Mama's way out of bondage. I saved every penny I earned and bought household items for a hope chest—not for myself, but for the day when Mama was free to start life over.

A big-box store, Carolina Pottery Outlet, stood right next door to Carowinds.

I got in the habit of saving as much as possible from what I earned at Carowinds, and when I had enough, I went next door and purchased items for Mama's new apartment that I believed she and I were going to have in Nashville when she made her escape from Daddy. I hid the items I purchased in a closet where Daddy was unlikely to find them.

Occasionally, when Mama found some of the utensils and towels I was hiding, she'd try to temper my hopes with a strong dose of reality. "Julie, you shouldn't be spending your money on something that may—"

"May what, Mama?" I'd interrupt. "May never happen? Oh, it's gonna happen, Mama. It's got to. Don't you give up."

I graduated from high school with highest honors. I really wanted to attend college somewhere in Nashville, but I didn't have enough money. So instead, I enrolled in community college at the University of South Carolina-Lancaster, not far from our home, where I could take my basic required courses less expensively. Both Mama and Marie had gone to USCL, so I realized the logic of going there.

Growing up, I thought I might want to major in music. But that changed when I auditioned for and was selected for a summer program at Winthrop University in Rock Hill, South Carolina, that focused on musical theater. It was my first introduction to Broadway-style musicals, and I liked it a lot, especially the close harmonies in the show tunes. I sang the lead in *My Fair Lady*, a part I had to sing with a cockney accent that shared little resemblance to the sounds of country music!

While at Winthrop, I realized I didn't want to major in music because most music majors pursued teaching careers rather than performing. I didn't want to teach music. Even a career in music therapy, which some of my counselors suggested because of my singing in nursing homes, brought me back to knowing more about music than performing music and getting involved in the music industry. I was much more interested in Belmont's music business program.

Because the degree had the word *business* attached, Daddy accepted the idea more readily. Daddy was a stickler for education, so I was surprised that he didn't discourage me from pursuing a degree in music business. Marie had wanted to major in dance, but Daddy refused to help her financially. He said, "I'm not helping you to get a degree in dance. You're going to break your legs, and you won't be able to make a living." I felt sad for Marie because she submerged her dream. She went to college to become an English teacher, and today she is an excellent high school assistant principal. But I can't help wondering whether she might have experienced more joy as a dancer.

Daddy tried that same tactic with me. He knew I was

good in math and science, so he challenged me, "You love animals, so why don't you be a veterinarian?"

"I do love animals, Daddy," I said, "but I can't stand to see them in pain. I don't want to be a vet. It's not what I love." For some reason, that assuaged his objections, or, perhaps, since he had already decided he wasn't going to help me pay for college, it simply didn't matter to him.

I attended USCL practically for free during my first two years of college. I studied hard and earned straight As, knowing I would need good grades to get scholarships, and I needed as much scholarship help as possible. I didn't waste time, money, or effort on classes that would not transfer to Belmont.

While attending the University of South Carolina-Lancaster, I took a class, The History of Country Music, taught by Pete Arnold, the retired dean of the college. Professor Arnold looked to be in his midsixties and was passionate about country music in an almost nostalgic, sentimental sort of way. He said things such as, "Country music is about being real. When you hear Hank Williams sing, you know you're hearing the truth." The course exposed me to the great heritage I wanted to become part of—country legends such as Loretta Lynn, the Carter Family, Tammy Wynette, and Patsy Cline.

Professor Arnold must have recognized that the sounds of traditional country music resonated with me. He invited me to sing with Rebecca's Dream, a band he formed that played acoustic country classics at Rotary clubs, university events, and small venues around Lancaster. We had no illusions about the band going big-time, but it was fantastic training and great experience in learning how to communicate with an audience solely with a song.

Planning to transfer to Belmont in Nashville for my junior year, I applied for the Vince Gill Scholarship, a popular award at Belmont funded by the country music superstar. I checked our mailbox at the end of the gravel driveway every day in anticipation of a reply. When a letter from Belmont finally arrived, I was almost too nervous to open it. Daddy was home at the time. I didn't tell him it had arrived but instead took the letter inside the house and placed it on the dining room table. I stared at the letter and worried that it might contain a negative response. When at last I worked up my courage, I picked up the envelope and slowly slid my finger under the flap. I pulled out an official-looking letter with a Curb School of Music Business header. I was ecstatic as I read, "You have been awarded the Vince Gill Scholarship." I immediately grabbed the phone and called Mama. I read her the letter, and we both quietly squealed with excitement— Mama trying to contain her joy at work, and me attempting to avoid interrupting Daddy. Although the amount of the award would pay only a small portion of Belmont's tuition, I was thrilled. To me, it was almost like a divine sign, pointing me toward Music City.

Daddy was working on his motorcycle in the garage when I received the letter announcing the scholarship. I was so excited, I ran into the garage and handed him the letter from Belmont. He read the letter and handed it back to me without a word, stooped down, and went back to work on his motorcycle.

"Aren't you going to say anything?" I asked. "Anything at all, like, 'Hey, Julie, you received a scholarship. I'm really proud of you.' Or something?"

Daddy slowly rose to his full stature. He wiped his hands on a greasy rag and said, "Yes, I'm proud of you, Julie. Haven't I always told you how smart you are? You've gotten straight As in school, even in math. With your brains, you could have a career in medicine, science, anything you want. Something useful. Something where you can make a good living."

"I want to be a singer, Daddy. Why can't you accept that?"

Daddy scowled and rolled his eyes. "You better come up with a plan B," he said.

"There is no plan B," I said. "I want to sing. I feel as though God created me to sing."

"Well, then God can pay the bill for you to sing too."

I was nineteen when I transferred to Belmont University and moved to Nashville. When I arrived at Belmont, I got a work-study job in the registrar's office, where the transcripts of students' grades were kept. It was a job with a lot of downtime, so I passed the time by browsing through the grades of famous former students.

Although the program has changed today, my music-business major involved three main areas: marketing, artist management, and recording classes. In the recording classes, I found a number of kindred spirits, including songwriters, musicians, and singers. It was only a short time before I gathered a group around me and we formed a band. The group was composed of five guys and me, so we called the band "Julie and the Not-So-Pretty Boys." We played current country radio hits and a few originals written by our band members. Just as Mr. Hargett, my guitar teacher, had promised, these musicians knew the Nashville number system and most were better guitar players than I was, so although I played my guitar onstage, I let the musicians carry the music while I focused on singing.

I hadn't written any songs before attending Belmont. But as my professors and fellow students constantly reminded me, "Writing songs is one of the best ways to make an impression and find inroads to a career in music." I was so naive about the music business, I didn't realize that many music stars did not write their own hit songs; in many cases, the songs had been written by professional songwriters. Other artists wrote only a portion of their own material, collaborating with professional songwriters. Garth Brooks, for example, reportedly quipped about writing sessions, "I just brought the beer that day, and my name is on that song."

None of the female vocalists I really loved and regarded as musical role models—Trisha Yearwood, Barbara Mandrell, Patsy Cline, and others—wrote their own hit songs, so I had not realized the importance of writing and singing my own material. Besides, I was much more concerned about singing songs that moved me than garnering a writing credit.

But after taking a class in publishing and copyright law at Belmont, I decided to try my hand at songwriting.

It didn't come naturally to me at first, but Casey Black, a student in one of my classes and a budding songwriter with a lot of ambition, offered to help me. Casey was the son of Charlie Black, a successful Nashville songwriter. Casey's dad had written hits for Anne Murray, Reba McEntire, and many others. Casey himself already had a publishing agreement with EMI Music, even while he was a student at Belmont. That meant he received a monthly allowance to write and record song demos. In return, he was required to turn in one new song each month to his publisher.

Casey helped me to write my first song—a song about Mama called "One Day My Someday Will Come." It wasn't a great song, but it was good enough that Casey was able to count it in his monthly quota. To me, it was a song Mama could sing about leaving Daddy. We recorded a demo of the song at Belmont. Nothing ever came of it, but I was now a songwriter.

"Hey, Julie, my dad is playing a writers-in-the-round show at the Bluebird Café," Casey told me one day. "I'm going to play some songs with him. Do you want to sing the song we wrote together?"

Casey didn't have to ask me twice.

The Bluebird Café is a small but famous venue in Nashville. It seats only about one hundred people, but it is known as a place where new writers and artists are discovered. Don

Schlitz, who wrote "The Gambler" for Kenny Rogers, was one of the first writers to appear there. Since then, artists such as Keith Urban, Kenny Chesney, Kix Brooks, John Oates, and more have joined writers-in-the-round shows. Garth Brooks and Kathy Mattea received record deals after their performances at the small club. In recent years, the Bluebird has grown even more popular due to its many scenes in the television program *Nashville*.

I was excited to be singing at the Bluebird. I felt sure I was going to be discovered that night. *I'm going to get a record deal tonight!* I thought, as I dressed in my jeans and the fanciest blouse in my college apartment closet. I curled my hair and did my makeup just as I had done many times at the theme parks where I had performed.

Casey's dad and a couple of other songwriters opened the writers-in-the-round show. This type of presentation is slightly different than usual performances. The songwriters sit in a circle with the audience surrounding them. Each writer takes turns introducing his or her song and explaining the story behind it. Then the writer performs the song, and usually the other writers will chime in on background vocals or other instruments.

Casey was one of the songwriters performing that night, so I sat behind him, to make maneuvering into the circle easier when they announced my name. As I sat up straight on the edge of my seat, my hands folded as I waited, I tried to pay attention to all the other writers, but I kept running the lyrics to my song over and over in my mind in anticipation of my own performance. I glanced around the room periodically, searching for anyone I might recognize in the music industry.

I had studied Nashville's hit makers, and I knew what most looked like. None were there—at least none that I saw. But that didn't calm my nerves at all. When I'm nervous, I tend to yawn, so I yawned quite a bit that night. People in the audience may have thought I was bored. I wasn't. I just wanted my first Bluebird performance to lead to my first big break.

When it was time for Casey and me to sing, Casey sat and played guitar, and I stood right next to him as we performed the first song we had written together, "One Day My Someday Will Come." I watched Casey's dad as we sang, and it was obvious from the expression on his face that he was pleased. That mattered a lot to me, because he was successful in the business. Casey and I did a good job on our song, and the crowd applauded politely. But I didn't get discovered or get a record deal that night. I was disappointed but determined. I knew I had to pay my dues, and I couldn't wait for the next opportunity.

Casey and I continued writing together, occasionally recording our songs after hours in his dad's writing studio on Music Row. Just walking into the office inspired me. Charlie Black's wall was covered with award plaques and framed gold albums featuring one or more of his songs.

Casey helped me to develop as a writer, teaching me the craft and collaborative process of songwriting and how to best put my ideas to music. I liked simple words and concepts. But Casey helped me to shape my lines in such a way that was simple but not predictable.

Later, I wrote with Cory Darling, one of the guys in my band. Cory worked at an entry-level job, answering phones for EMI Music. He was a great guy I had met at Belmont, and we quickly discovered we shared a love for country music. Cory was well organized and approached music in a very business-like manner. We became great friends, and because we spent so much time together writing songs and working with the band, we gradually grew into a dating relationship as well.

I loved being at Belmont, working toward my dream, and meeting talented people such as Casey and Cory, but not everything was rosy. Belmont regularly hosted potential artist showcase performances. To be granted a spot on the schedule, musicians, bands, and singers had to enter an audition tape that was then given feedback from the showcase committee. I submitted one tape after another, but I was never selected to perform.

One of the committee members wrote on my advice sheet, "You should stick to songwriting rather than singing."

I called Mama crying my eyes out. Mama reminded me that, similar to my high school chorus teacher, not everyone is going to get what I do. "Are you going to allow one person's opinion to change your path?" Mama asked. I realized afresh that overcoming doubters was going to be part of the life I'd chosen. And sometimes even the best experts are wrong.

I'm glad I followed Mama's advice rather than the experts'.

5

Comings and Goings

$\mathcal{N}$obody starts at the top in any line of work, and gaining experience usually requires a lot of hard work and sacrifice. Between my junior and senior years at Belmont, I got a job working in a musical revue at Dollywood, the fabulous, family-friendly theme park developed by country music icon Dolly Parton in Pigeon Forge, Tennessee, near Gatlinburg and the Great Smoky Mountains. My purpose in working there during the summer was to save money for my tuition the following year. But my expenses were more than I anticipated. For one thing, Dollywood had fantastic food, and I ate at their bakery—a lot! I was living by myself, so I was also paying for an apartment lease and for my Honda. The apartment complex was rather shady and scary, and I could hear people fighting next door. I wedged a chair under the doorknob to my front entry every night before going to bed.

As part of the cast of *Country Treasures* at Dollywood, I performed four shows every day and five shows a day on weekends, including a set with an established Grand Ole Opry star. Because of Dolly's reputation, we had many great artists come through, and I was always impressed with how kind they were to the young members of our show cast, almost all of whom hoped to make it in the music business. Jeannie Seely was especially friendly to me. Jeannie made it a point to meet every performer in the show, offering words of encouragement. When she came to me, she complimented me on my performance, and I responded cheerily, "Thank you, Jeannie. Someday I'm going to sing with you on the Opry!" Jeannie smiled. I was sure she had heard that a million times, but she didn't disagree.

Our young, energetic troupe put on a nonstop country music show, singing and dancing all over the stage. One of the dance routines called for me to leap above the head of one of the male dancers. I made the jump okay, but unfortunately, the guy dropped me. I hit the floor hard. That ended my dancing for a while, but I was still able to sing in the show, while sitting on a haystack.

Later that summer, I heard about another singing job opening in a show at Carowinds, where I could live at home and save more money. I auditioned and got the job. Similar to the Dollywood schedule, we did four shows each day and five shows on weekends, so the good news was that I didn't have to pay for an apartment. The bad news? I wasn't home very much.

I kept the job at Carowinds throughout my senior year of college, performing mostly on weekends. Often, I drove all the way to North Carolina, did the shows at Carowinds, and then raced back across Tennessee on Interstate 40, completing the nearly nine-hundred-mile round trip to arrive back at Belmont in time for Monday morning classes.

The guys in my Belmont band were typical musicians—we'd play anywhere! We played at dubious venues such as Guido's Pizza Shop, Bongo Java coffee shop, and even Harvey Washbanger's, a Laundromat! Of course, every so often during one of our songs, announcements came over the PA system: "Dryer number three is now open," or "Someone left a red thong in dryer number one."

We weren't embarrassed to be playing such nondescript venues; we were proud! Many small restaurants, bars, and shops in Nashville featured live music, and these rooms were sometimes used as showcases for new artists. Stories abound of wannabe artists discovered at small clubs in Nashville—as I mentioned, a music executive first heard Garth Brooks sing at the Bluebird Café and signed him to a record deal, and Randy Travis was discovered at the Nashville Palace, where he had washed dishes!

I worked my way through school and graduated from Belmont University with a degree in music business in 2001. My whole family—even Daddy—attended the ceremony. I hugged Daddy tightly and thanked him for coming. It meant the world to me that he came to my graduation. It was one of the few times in my life that I felt he was proud of me.

I experienced a mix of emotions at my college graduation. I was anxious about what might come next, but I was also excited about my future and especially pleased that I had made Mama happy by earning a college degree. Even Daddy seemed satisfied that I now had a business degree to "fall back on." But I had no intention of falling back. I was ready to move forward toward my dream. I had no doubt that it would come to pass—somehow.

While still in school, I had worked as an unpaid intern at Sony Music. I also had a paid internship at Universal Music, working in the mailroom, floating between departments, doing whatever needed to be done, and hoping that one of my internships might lead to a full-time job at a record company. Shortly after I graduated, a receptionist position opened at Mercury Records. "Would you be interested in applying for that job?" my boss at Universal asked.

Would I be interested? You bet! It was a fantastic opportunity to get my foot in the door, and I needed a job to support myself as an aspiring country music artist. Plus, I loved the idea of being surrounded by the creativity and energy of a record company, so this was the ideal employment for me. I knew how hard it was to get such a position in the music business. Many of my fellow graduates were working outside the industry, hoping to find some way to get in, and here I was with an open door right in front of me.

I got the job at Mercury and worked as a receptionist in the main lobby. At the time, Luke Lewis served as cochairman and CEO, basically the head of the Mercury label. An energetic executive in his midfifties, Luke was equally as comfortable wearing a baseball cap and jeans as he was a suit and tie. But his informality belied the truth that he ran a tight operation with high expectations. Luke could be curt and brusque, but he was nice to me, and I quickly grew to admire and respect him.

For the next two years, I spent my days answering phones at Mercury and filled my nights with music, honing my songwriting skills and performing at various clubs around Music City.

Mark Wright headed up the MCA label at the time. Then the labels merged under Universal, and Luke told me, "Mark wants you to be his receptionist." The two record companies were next door to each other, so I still worked in the same area but had a different boss.

Besides scheduling Mark's appointments and taking care of his artists, my duties also included having Mark's coffee ready for him when he arrived at the office. He liked his coffee a certain light-brown color, with a specific coffee creamer. I did everything I could to please him. One day, I noticed the coffee creamer's "use before" date was expired. I called Mama and told her. "That's no problem," she said. "Just take your pen and change that date, and quit worrying about it."

I did, and when Mark came in, I handed him his coffee.

He thanked me and said, "You're gonna make somebody a great wife someday."

My face flushed red. "I don't want to be a great wife," I fired back. "I want to be a great singer." I walked out of Mark's office. I appreciated Mark's compliment, but being a great wife was not on my front burner.

A short time later, Luke Lewis became the chairman of Universal Music Group Nashville, now the parent company of Mercury and MCA, which meant he was now Mark's boss. The company's human resources officer came by my desk and said, "Luke would like you to be his assistant if you are interested."

To be Luke's label assistant would be a promotion, and I would receive an increase in pay, so I said, "Sure!"

"Well, there's one stipulation," the HR person said. "And that is that you *not* be an aspiring singer. If you are a singer, then don't tell us. Luke doesn't want someone working in this position who is trying to be a country music artist."

I took the job, but I carefully made sure my two worlds never collided. It was an awkward situation. Working as Luke's assistant meant I sat daily just a few feet away from the man who could make all my dreams come true—but I never said a word to him about my desires. He was the head of the music company; I was his assistant, answering the phone, talking with agents and artists' managers, and making appointments for other potential superstars, all the while working at my desk located right outside Luke's door.

I didn't dare let on that I was a singer or that I was writing songs and recording demos down the street from our office. I had heard rumors that Luke had fired employees in our office who had the audacity to bring him a demo tape of songs they had recorded.

"Send me a demo, and I'll send you a pink slip," he quipped.

With my increased salary, I immediately started making plans for Mama to move to Nashville. "We're gonna get you a job, and you can move here and live with me," I told her.

Mama wasn't so certain. She was fearful about starting life over again at fifty years of age. Moreover, Mama had lived in the same town all her life, and most of her family members still lived nearby. She wasn't real sure she wanted to move to a new location. But she prayed about it as I searched online for job opportunities in Nashville. I found a local company that manufactured mattresses, and they needed someone with accounting experience. I felt that might be a godsend, so I sent them an application on Mama's behalf. Not only did they respond quickly, but they also invited Mama to fly to Nashville for an interview at the company's expense! It seemed almost too good to be true.

Mama was excited to visit Nashville so she and I could spend some time together, but she also prayed seriously about the job opportunity before she went to the interview. Her prayer sounded something like, "Lord, if I'm supposed to move here, I need to get a job offer today."

That same day, before she left the interview, the human resources officer offered her a job as an accountant for the mattress company. "Okay," she said. "I'll take it."

No doubt, leaving was emotionally wrenching for Mama. But Marie was already married and Lorie was off to college. And Daddy was . . . well, Daddy. There was nothing holding Mama back anymore.

She divorced Daddy. Leaving with only what she could carry, Mama loaded up her 1991 Ford Escort and, along with her dog, Dixie, started driving toward Nashville.

I imagined Mama looking in the rearview mirror, hoping that Daddy wasn't following her. I encouraged her to keep her eyes focused on what was ahead, but even that seemed scary for Mama. What sort of future did she have? Her whole life was packed into that beat-up, old car.

"I know it's hard, Mama," I said, "but you can't look back." I hated to think about her driving out there in the middle of nowhere along Interstate 40. I prayed the entire time: *Please, God, don't let her break down along the road. If she's gonna break down physically or emotionally, let her break down here.*

When Mama arrived, we laughed and cried. She had done it! She had made a clean break from Daddy. After living half a century, she was ready to start enjoying her life. For the first time since she married at twenty-five years of age, she could wear makeup and the pretty red dresses that Daddy never allowed her to wear during their marriage. I was glad she was courageous enough to take a chance.

At first, she and I got an apartment together. Eventually, Mama's income combined with mine provided enough that she was able to purchase a lovely townhome on the west side of Nashville. I unpacked all the "hope chest" items I had bought for Mama and gave them to her. We both had trouble holding back our tears.

6

Some Risks Are Worth It

I was still writing and performing with Cory Darling, my boyfriend from Belmont. He worked at EMI Music, which was also home to Brent Rowan, a veteran recording-session guitarist and producer. Brent had worked with Tim McGraw, Toby Keith, and Neil Diamond and had recently produced a huge hit record with Joe Nichols, an EMI writer. I knew Brent because he occasionally brought in new artists for Luke Lewis to meet or other projects for Luke to hear.

Casually but conservatively dressed, with sandy hair and glasses, Brent did not fit the image of a big-time Nashville producer. He wore Wrangler jeans, pressed Western-style shirts, and boots. To me, he looked more like a cowboy than a musical genius. He didn't act like some of the more arrogant producers or artist managers who often came in yelling at Luke about some injustice their artist was enduring. Instead, Brent was always courteous and kind, taking time to greet me pleasantly before going in to meet with Luke.

Cory took some of our band songs to Brent. "I play music at night with this girl and a band from school," he said, "and we recorded this. Do you want to listen to it? You know her. She's a receptionist over at Mercury."

A few days later, Brent Rowan called me at Mercury. "Cory gave me a tape of the songs you and the band recorded," he said. "I hate the music, but I love your voice."

"Really?" I said. I was disappointed that Brent didn't like our band, but I was really excited that he liked my singing. "So what does that mean?" I asked.

"I know you are playing these Laundromat gigs," Brent said, "but if you will put them on hold for a while, let's try to record some songs. I have access to a basement studio at EMI after business hours, so we can do some guitar and vocal demos after you get off work."

"Yessss!" I said. "I've been wanting to stop playing Laundromats for a long, long time!" I wasn't worried about the inevitable clash between my day job and my secret career aspirations, because we'd be working together when it was unlikely that I'd run into any of the EMI executives who frequented Luke's office.

I had been going to the Bluebird Café listening for new songs, and one night, songwriter Jason Matthews presented a new song he'd written with Jess Brown called "Break Down Here." As I listened, the song ripped at my heart and I could barely keep the tears from trickling down my face. The poignant lyrics about a person who was escaping a bad relationship sounded as though the writers were describing Mama's life.

That's it. I can connect with those lyrics, I thought. *I have to get ahold of this song and play it for Brent.* Sure enough, "Break Down Here" was the first song Brent and I recorded together.

Cory found some great songs at EMI, and Brent had a collection of songs written by some established writers in town, so between us, we found and recorded five songs that we felt good about. It didn't happen overnight. Just the opposite; it took months and months to find the songs we wanted and to get them recorded well enough to present to record companies. At long last, Brent felt we were ready.

Brent took our demos to several labels around town, and the response was the same everywhere he went: rejection. "It's too bluesy," some labels said. "It's too soulful," others said. All the labels Brent approached said no. I was down and discouraged, but Brent always found a way to bring me back up. "Don't worry," he said. "Don't give up. We'll find somebody who gets this."

I trusted Brent, and I trusted in God's timing.

One day, Brent said, "I want to take our demos to Luke."

"No, Brent," I said. "You'll get me fired. I'm not supposed to be a singer. Remember? I have school loans to pay; I have a car payment and a mortgage. If I lose my job, are you going to pay those?"

"Just get me on his calendar," Brent said. "I'll take it from there."

A few days later, I nervously approached my boss, making an extra effort to appear professional and nonchalant. "Brent Rowan is working with a new artist in town," I said, "and he would like to schedule a meeting with you."

Luke knew Brent and was aware of his success as a producer and respected him. He didn't even blink. He didn't ask whether Brent's new artist was male or female. He simply said, "Sure, find a spot on my calendar and book it."

I breathed a sigh of relief and quickly found an open appointment on Luke's schedule that I could give to Brent.

The day came, and Brent showed up at the office. He greeted me casually, with a twinkle in his eye, but he did not give any indication that we knew each other in any other capacity. I informed Luke that Brent had arrived, and my stomach whirled like a Tilt-A-Whirl at an amusement park.

Brent went in Luke's office, and they closed the door. After a few minutes Brent played some of the demos he and I recorded, but he had assured me beforehand that he would not tell Luke whose voice he was hearing.

Luke liked to listen to music loudly, so I could hear my own voice through the wall separating my desk from Luke's office, but I couldn't tell whether Luke liked the music. I had worked with Luke for more than two years. I knew how these meetings went. If the music didn't pique Luke's interest, then Brent wouldn't be in there long.

With each passing minute, my heart thumped wildly.

When the music stopped, I thought my own heart would stop as well.

The music started again—then stopped. Then started and stopped at least five more times.

Oh, no, I thought, *he didn't like it*. I felt as though I might pass out.

When Brent finally came out, he didn't say anything to me. I tried my best not to look at him as he said goodbye to Luke. I couldn't tell if the meeting had gone well or poorly!

Before leaving, Brent whispered, "Call me when you get off work." I nodded.

It was near the end of business hours, and Luke soon left the office. His only words to me were, "I'll see you tomorrow."

Now I was really worried. Surely if Luke had liked the demos, he would have said something. As soon as I was sure my boss was gone, I called Brent.

Brent told me what had happened. He had played three song demos without telling Luke that it was me singing. After the third song, the music mogul punched Pause on the recorder and asked to know the name of the artist. "I love that voice," Luke said. "Who is this woman? I want to meet her. I like her."

Brent smiled. "She's right outside your door."

"What?"

"You're listening to your assistant."

"What assistant?"

Brent pointed toward the hallway. "That's Julie," he said with a smile.

"You're kidding me." Luke Lewis was flabbergasted and

let loose a litany of expletives expressing his surprise. "She's not supposed to be a singer!" he said.

"I know," Brent replied. "But she is . . . and a good one too."

Brent assured me that Luke had liked our demos, but he advised me to lie low until Luke committed, so for the next few days, I lived in limbo, not knowing for sure what Luke was going to do.

Finally, after several days, Luke approached me. "I heard your stuff," he said curtly. "And I like it."

"And?"

"I now know that you want to be an artist, not a record label assistant. So here's what we're going to do. Don't say anything to anyone. I am going to play your demos for the other decision makers around the company, but I'm not going to tell them it is you. If they respond positively, then we'll move forward; we will sign you to Mercury. If they don't like it, then I won't ever tell them that it is you; we'll forget this ever happened, and you can keep your job here." A hint of a smile creased Luke's face.

"Thank you, Luke," I said. My heart started racing again, and I could feel my face getting red. I smiled back at my boss and said, "I like that plan."

It was several more days before Luke brought in the verdict. As usual, Luke maintained his matter-of-fact manner. "I need a new assistant," he said. "We're going to sign you to a record deal."

"Yeessssss!" I squealed.

"And the new assistant *cannot* be a singer!" Luke said with a broad smile.

Luke went back in his office, and as soon as possible, I called Mama. "It's happened, Mama," I said, jumping up and down as I nearly screamed into the telephone. "I got a record deal! Can you believe it, Mama? It finally happened!"

"Oh, Julie, I knew it would!" Mama sounded as though she was jumping up and down, too, but I couldn't tell whether she was laughing or crying, or maybe a bit of both.

"It's my dream, Mama . . . our dream . . . and we're gonna live it together!"

7

In Production

True to his word, a few weeks later, Luke presented me a deal with Mercury Records for not merely one album but *seven* albums! We gathered in the Mercury conference room for a formal signing ceremony, complete with media photographers and television cameras filming as I signed my name to the agreement.

"All right," Luke said with a grin. "Go make your record." He gave Brent Rowan a free hand to produce the album, and our agreement provided the necessary money to pay for Brent, the musicians, engineers, studio time, and even for meals. The only person who wouldn't get paid was me! Not until the album "recouped"—in other words, sold enough copies that the record company had earned back all the money it had put into the recording and promoting process—would I begin to earn royalties. Regardless of the financial strains I might endure in the short term, I was thrilled. I was making a record!

And I found Luke a new receptionist, my friend Erin Mason, who promised me that she did not want to be a singer.

Almost immediately, my life became a blur of activity. In January 2004, Brent and I went back to work finishing the songs for my first album. We still had at least five more songs to find and record. That meant hour after hour in listening sessions, searching for potential hit songs that spoke to me lyrically.

Once we got back in the studio, Brent wanted to keep the same vibe we had achieved on the demos he had pitched to Luke. Brent was brilliant, too, knowing exactly what he wanted to do musically before going into each recording session, rather than spending gobs of money sitting around hoping for creativity to strike. Because he was so well prepared, we recorded the instrumental tracks for the entire album in less than five days.

He hired Gary Paczosa, a fantastic engineer who had worked on hit records with Alison Krauss, Dolly Parton, and other female artists. Brent wanted Gary's expertise in recording a female voice, so he encouraged Gary to "set the board," setting the equalization and other important functions of the mixing board. Brent focused more on the content of the music and let Gary tend to the technical aspects. They made a good team.

We recorded most of my vocals at Gary's West Nashville studio, the Doghouse. Usually, after Gary set up the console, he would leave. Brent and I were the only ones there. Since there weren't any onlookers from the record label looming over our shoulders in the studio, the atmosphere was really low-key. I wasn't nervous at all, and I enjoyed the recording process.

Brent's calm personality helped too. He never griped, complained, or grew impatient. If something wasn't right, we simply fixed it.

"For me, music comes down to two things," he said. "Either I believe it or I don't. And with you, I believe it."

That became our standard. Regardless of whether the notes were right or a musical riff needed to be rejected or added, Brent listened intently to my voice.

When he said, "Okay, I believe it," I knew we had a keeper.

Because I had formerly worked on the inside of the record label, I knew what some producers and artists were spending on their albums. Most artists rarely worried about the enormous bills they racked up, paid by the record company but applied against the artists' future royalties. Producers had similar deals, but their recoupment was not based on the artists' exorbitant expenses.

Brent was extremely frugal. He didn't waste money on

frivolous expenses such as catering food to the studio while we recorded. Instead, we called out for fast food. Brent brought in the entire record, including the final mastering process, under budget. Luke Lewis was duly impressed. He hadn't seen an album expense sheet like that in a long time!

Besides "Break Down Here," I especially loved "Rain on a Tin Roof," a song about a guy who keeps dropping in and out of a woman's life. His love is like rain on a tin roof—invigorating and refreshing, but he runs off quickly, and you never know when he's coming back. "Wake Up Older" was a gritty song about self-destructive behavior after a love was over and a guy walked out; the recording session was emotional, and the song came out great.

One of my favorite songs on the album, "The Chance," was especially meaningful to me. The lyrics told a story of a woman who had poured her life into her child, forgoing her own dreams to give the child opportunities to live, to explore, and to risk. Consequently, the child cannot sit on the sidelines of life but is committed to dancing every dance, while the chance remained.

During the recording of the song, Brent turned down the lights in the studio where I was singing and in the control room where he was sitting, monitoring the board. I closed my eyes and sang my heart out. By the end of the song, I was crying.

Brent came out of the control room and hugged me. "It's okay," he said. "I believe you."

Again, I felt through the lyrics the sacrifice Mama had made for me, giving up so much of her life so I could live out my dreams. The song motivated me to get moving, even on those days when I was down, discouraged, or not feeling well. I didn't want to miss a single dance. And I owed it to Mama to take advantage of every opportunity, to make the most of today, while I still had the chance. As I recorded the song, I had no idea that I was describing my future.

Songwriters Paul Overstreet and Jason Matthews wrote "Unlove Me," another special but sad song about loosing the ties that bind, undoing all the things that made two people fall in love. I loved the song, but for some reason, I couldn't remember the words. I wondered at times if there might be something wrong with my brain, causing the glitches in my memory.

The song had been on hold for a new artist on another label, Miranda Lambert, who had made a huge splash on the television show *Nashville Star*. I wanted to record the song, so the publishers went back to Miranda's producers and asked, "Is she going to record it? If not, we have somebody who will record it tomorrow." Miranda's producer released the hold on the song, and I went in and recorded it the next day.

Brent arranged for some guest artists to help me on the album by singing background vocals on select songs. He had Delbert McClinton sing background vocals on "No Way Out," and Pat McLaughlin did a super job on "Break Down Here." But I could not have imagined the artist he invited to sing on "Unlove Me" and "The Chance."

"Vince Gill is coming in to sing some background vocals tomorrow," Brent told me one evening before I left the studio. I could hardly believe it! I had never met Vince, but it was the Vince Gill Scholarship that had helped get me to Nashville.

I got all dressed up the next day and sat in the studio, nervously waiting for the superstar to arrive. I called Mama at her workplace and told her, "Mama, Vince Gill is coming to the studio today."

"What? No way!" Both Mama and I were huge Vince Gill fans. (Mama wanted to marry Vince!) In addition to being incredibly talented, Vince always came across as a really nice man. We had attended his concert in South Carolina, and I had been starstruck ever since.

I knew that Vince and his wife, Amy Grant, lived on the west side of Nashville, but I was nonetheless surprised when Vince arrived at the studio on a bicycle. He was wearing black biking shorts, a black T-shirt, and a helmet.

There I was, all glammed up in my dress and high heels.

"Hey, I'm Vince," he said, extending his hand to shake mine. "Pardon my appearance. I love donuts, but I want to lose a few pounds. That's why I ride my bike so much these days."

We talked briefly, and Vince asked, "What are we singing today?"

Brent played the songs for Vince, and he picked up on his harmony parts immediately. Brent had a good idea what he wanted Vince to sing, without overdoing it, so it didn't take Vince long to add his voice to mine.

"Is that okay?" Vince asked, looking at me.

"It's awesome," I said. In my mind, I was saying, *Of course it's okay! You are Vince Gill!*

"I love your record," Vince said as he retrieved his biking

helmet and we said goodbye. Vince got on his bike and rode away, leaving behind his incredible vocal performance.

Even though I had worked at Mercury for more than two years, I was still surprised at just how many people are involved in launching the career of a new, relatively unknown artist. Besides working closely with Brent in the studio, I now had what seemed like an army of people offering their wisdom, advice, and direction about my career. Mercury helped me find a manager, Ron Shapiro, a former executive with Atlantic Records. Ron's offices were in New York, but he kept a finger on the pulse of Music City as well. He knew the business inside and out, and he seemed excited about helping me develop a long-standing career in country music. Working closely with Ron was my concert booking agent, Ron Baird of Creative Artists Agency, with whom I also signed a deal, and Jason Owen, the vice president of artist media relations for Mercury.

Eventually, I would have a full-time radio promotions team, whose job it was to help get my first single played by radio stations across the country. That is no easy task, especially when there is so much new music for radio program directors and deejays to pick from. Each week, most major country radio stations add two songs and drop two songs from their active playlists—the songs the program directors and deejays agree to play—in regular rotation. In any given week, a station receives fifty or more new singles from established record companies and small, independent companies, all vying for those same two open positions. It is intensely competitive, so Mercury wanted to do everything possible to help me nab a spot in the active rotation on radio station playlists all around the country.

One of the early coups in the advance promotion of my album happened when Jason Owen landed a feature on Country Music Television (CMT). I would be the first artist to appear in the network's premiere of *In the Moment*, a behind-the-scenes documentary and reality-style program in which the network would follow me, hopefully tracking my rise from obscurity to country music stardom—from behind my desk as the receptionist in Luke's office to the release of my first album. The show would include the very beginning of my career, from the recording studio to the efforts to convince radio stations to play my music, to the early stages of success. The cameras and production staff would be a perpetual presence in my life for the next six months or so. While it seemed terribly intrusive, I was excited about the potential exposure.

As the vice president of artist media relations, Jason Owen was the head of public relations at Mercury. He had helped direct the hugely successful publicity campaign for Shania Twain, who was well known for both her great voice and her great body. Jason focused a lot of attention on an artist's image, so perhaps that was why he demanded that I go to "boot camp" before going out to promote my music.

The label's boot camp was an intense eight-week program

focusing on diet and exercise. Fortunately, I enjoy working out, but it really wasn't optional. My record label demanded that I fit into the image they were creating for me. I met my trainer to work out five days a week, each morning at six o'clock. Apparently he didn't know that most musicians think that six o'clock comes only once a day!

I would do an hour of cardio workouts early in the morning, then my trainer often wanted me to come back again later in the day for another hour of cardio. Looming largely in front of me as motivation was a calendar with my promotional photo-shoot schedule on it.

I began my boot camp weighing about 138 pounds. That's not fat by any means, but it isn't the look the label wanted either. The label wanted me to weigh in at 108 pounds, so I went to the gym every day. After sixteen weeks, I had lost more than twenty pounds.

The label wanted me to eat only eight hundred calories per day. My trainer decided my daily calorie, protein, and total fat intake. I was required to keep a food journal, listing every single thing I put in my mouth each day, including drinks, fruit, snacks, breath mints—anything at all.

I did as I was told, and I made the goal the label had set for me. At the time, I wanted to do anything necessary to get my album out, but I certainly wasn't happy about not eating anything fun. I felt the dietary program was excessive, but if that's what it took for me to look the way my label preferred, I was willing. I assumed that was just part of the territory. I knew I was getting too thin for my size, though, when one of the label's radio reps looked at me and said, "You need to eat a cheeseburger."

Jamey Johnson and I were on the same label. Jamey is a big guy, but he was not overweight—at least not by most people's standards. It was obvious that he was not into exercise when he came to an abs class wearing a camouflage shirt and blue jeans instead of workout clothes. I saw him on the floor doing some crunches, so I stopped to say hello. "They have you in boot camp too?" I asked.

"Yep, and this is the last time you'll ever see me here," Jamey said. "I ain't comin' back."

I laughed, but I understood.

I knew that the PR department was trying to develop an image for me, similar to what they had created for Shania Twain, but it was getting ridiculous. I didn't even feel that I could go out to eat at a restaurant. When I did, I ordered egg whites and raw broccoli. That was all I was supposed to eat. Yuck!

Years later, I heard Grammy-winning artist Adele during an interview on *60 Minutes*. She was asked if she felt intimidated by the thinner female artists. "No," Adele replied. "I don't want to be skinny Minnie." I loved her candid comment and her courage to buck the system.

On the other hand, I appreciated the new "me" the handlers were helping to create. I wore new clothes and had better makeup. For a while, the record label even debated about giving me a new name. The label execs seriously wondered if the comparisons between my name and that of a certain famous actress might create confusion in the marketplace.

They never asked my opinion, but I'd sometimes joke, "Well, maybe Julia Roberts ought to change *her* name!"

Universal wanted to promote the idea that I was single and available, so they did not want me to mention that I had a boyfriend, much less that Cory and I had been dating for more than a year when I signed my record deal. "It's all about the image," they said. I willingly went along with the ruse, partly because I wanted to keep Cory's and my relationship private, but also because that's what the label's "product control" demanded. And I was the product they were developing.

8

In the Moment

*H*it records don't happen by accident. Even if the music is fantastic, it still takes an enormous amount of time, work, and promotional dollars to create a sufficient advertising buzz that will cause radio stations to play a new song by a new artist. To overcome these formidable obstacles, Jason Owen and his team sent me out on a six-week radio tour, traveling from one radio station to another promoting my first single, "Break Down Here." The entire album was not scheduled to release until May 2004, but we began the radio tour in February.

The radio tour was one of the most intense, exhausting, yet exhilarating experiences of my life. I was accompanied by three staff members from Mercury, as well as a guitar player and a keyboard guy, so we could do miniconcerts at each radio station and perform live during every broadcast. Mercury leased a luxurious tour bus to transport our team. A production crew from Country Music Television traveled on the bus with us, filming my every move for *In the Moment*. It was a massive and expensive undertaking, all to promote one song, which would hopefully lead to interest in my entire album.

We began the tour at WKDF-FM in Nashville, where we visited with Eddie Foxx, one of Music City's most popular morning deejays. After talking with me about the song on air for a few minutes, Eddie debuted "Break Down Here" on his show. I was so excited I could hardly stand it, listening to my own voice on the radio station broadcasting all over town. It felt surreal, but it wasn't. It was real. My dream was coming true! For a moment, I choked up and thought I might lose it emotionally.

I called Mama at work, where she was listening at her desk along with two of her coworkers. The CMT *In the Moment* cameraman was there, too, hoping to catch Mama's reaction on film. I could hear my song in the background, as I excitedly asked Mama, "How does it sound?"

Mama could barely speak, and I could tell that she was crying.

"Okay, I'll call ya later," I promised.

I looked to Haley McLemore, the representative from Mercury accompanying me, who was standing nearby in the radio station studio. "I'm glad I'm not there," I said. "I'd be crying right along with Mama!"

From Nashville, we made our way across the country,

stopping at several radio stations each day. Our goal at each stop was to get the radio station to add my single to its playlist and to keep my song in its regular rotation.

At every location, I signed advance photos of the album cover for everyone who wanted one. I signed autographs until my hand got sore. I even signed one buff guy's bare chest with a silver Sharpie. (It made sense at the time.)

At several stops along the way, Luke Lewis and Jason Owen flew out to join us. That the CEO of the record company and head of media would personally visit with radio personnel was a huge statement of support on behalf of our record.

By April, we were working night and day to promote the record, surviving on less than four hours of sleep each night, and waking up in a different city each day. It was a rigorous trip, requiring me to be up early each morning and at my best, hoping to make a good first impression on radio personnel, many of whom were hearing my music for the first time.

So much was riding on this tour, and at times I found myself battling nerves. *Everything is in God's hands,* I reminded myself. *When you stop believing in yourself, that's when the devil works on you.*

Despite our rigorous schedule, we were encountering a serious problem. Not enough new radio stations were adding "Break Down Here," and others weren't giving the record enough spins to move it up the charts.

Luke was concerned. He knew we had a good record, and he believed in it. "We've got our shot," he told his staff. "We don't want to miss this opportunity. It won't come around again. It's as good as it has ever been."

Jason felt that it was time to do something radical. He had secured a highly coveted photo shoot in *Maxim*, a magazine known primarily for its seductive photographs of actresses, music artists, and top models. The magazine claimed to have a circulation of more than nine million readers, mostly males.

Jason had already secured featured placements in *People, Ladies' Home Journal,* and *Glamour.* But I'd never done anything like *Maxim.* Jason felt it was a real coup for a country music artist to be featured in that publication.

Although the magazine would not pay me for the shoot, Jason suggested the idea to my manager, Ron Shapiro. Ron tried to put some boundaries around the photo shoot, regarding what type of photos the magazine could take.

I still wasn't sure, so I expressed my concerns. "I don't know about this, Jason," I told my PR expert. I had seen the magazine in airports and was aware that *Maxim* was considered edgy, but I had never even looked inside its cover. So I was extremely nervous about associating my name with it. On the way to the photo shoot in New York, I said to my manager, "I'm not comfortable with this, Ron." I was ready to cancel the shoot. Ron suggested that I talk with Luke in Nashville.

I called Luke, and he reassured me that the photographers could not push me to do risqué pictures. They were looking for more of a Daisy Duke effect. "I think you should do it," Luke said.

When we arrived at the studio, everyone was friendly and highly professional. No one pressured me in any way, although the stylist who was helping to choose outfits for me suggested a few looks that were more provocative than I would accept. "No way," I said, and Jason conveyed the message.

Jason stayed for the entire shoot as my protector and to make sure the photographer did not violate my standards. I wore denim shorts with a low-cut tank top that partially exposed my push-up bra as I was lying next to a guitar. They also used a shot of me with my denim jacket partially open. Although tastefully done and remarkably tame by many modeling standards nowadays, the photos nonetheless stretched my boundaries. After all, I was a Bible-believing Christian with an old-fashioned sense of morality.

Was I foolish and naive? Absolutely. But at the time, I was so gullible and obsessed with succeeding in the music business that I would have done almost anything my record label personnel suggested. Of course, they had my best interests at heart, didn't they? Besides, I trusted Jason completely. If he felt that I should do it, I would do it.

Unfortunately, at that point in my career, I had no control over what photos the magazine used, and I didn't see them until they were published in the magazine's seven-page spread.

Following the *Maxim* shoot, *Playboy* magazine approached the label wanting me to do a similar photo shoot and offering to pay me a lot of money. Jason firmly rebuffed them, letting them know that I had no intention to ever do such a thing.

Still hoping to secure more prerelease publicity, Luke was adamant with our promotions team that we had to keep working hard. "We could lose this record," he said, "at any given moment."

I tried to reassure myself that our efforts were not going to be in vain. "God got me this far, and he's not going to leave me now," I told several people on our team.

Luke, on the other hand, grew more frustrated with each passing day that radio stations did not aggressively play our record. "We've put a million dollars in this thing," he fretted, "and radio stations won't give us three minutes."

I continued to encourage everyone as best I could. "Everyone is working hard," I said, "and it is going to happen. In God's time, it is going to happen!"

The highlight of the tour and the apex of my career so far was making my first appearance on the Grand Ole Opry. I took in every detail as I walked through the famed artists' entryway behind the building, stopping at the security desk to give them my name and to receive my dressing room assignment. I peeked in every dressing room as I walked by, imagining Patsy Cline, Tammy Wynette, Merle Haggard, and so many other country stars getting ready in those rooms before walking out onto the storied Opry stage.

And now here I was! Julie Roberts, from Lancaster, South Carolina, getting ready to perform on that same prestigious platform. I had to pinch myself to make sure I wasn't dreaming!

Prior to the show, Mama and Lorie joined me backstage in my dressing room. Mawmaw was there too. She had made the four-hundred-fifty-mile trip from Lancaster just so she could be with me at this momentous event in my life. This was, after all, the Grand Ole Opry! It took all the self-control we could muster to contain our excitement. We had been hoping and praying for this opportunity for years, and now it was about to happen!

In a stark contrast to the more exotic photographs of me in the magazines, for the Opry, I wore a simple, country-style red shirt with white trim, black jeans, and boots. Not only was it a coast-to-coast live radio show in front of a crowd of nearly four thousand people, but the Opry was also home to my musical heroes, and I was getting ready to step onto that historic stage and stand in that circle behind the WSM microphone. I wanted to look respectable!

"How do I look, Mama?" I asked her at least a dozen times.

"You look great," she responded. "Quit askin' me!" We both laughed, easing the tension momentarily.

As a special treat, I had asked Brent Rowan to play guitar with me for my Opry debut of "Break Down Here." He stopped at my dressing room before we went onstage. I was more nervous than I'd ever been. "It's going to be great, Julie," Brent reassured me. "Everybody who played on the record will be onstage with you tonight. Have fun and enjoy this moment. Just be you."

I hugged Brent and thanked him again for his encouragement. Before we left the dressing room, Mawmaw, Mama,

Brent, Lorie, and I paused long enough to pray, thanking God for this incredible opportunity and asking him to calm my nerves! We moved as a unit behind the curtain, and I stood pensively in the dark, off stage right. Although the crowd couldn't see me, I could see and hear them in the backstage television monitor. The building was packed.

Whispering Bill Anderson, a country music icon, introduced me for my first performance on the Opry. Bill said in his introduction that I would never forget that moment, and I knew he was right.

A member of the stage crew handed me a microphone as I walked briskly onto the stage. I made certain that I stopped right in the middle of the famed wooden circle in the stage flooring. That circle of hardwood had been part of the original Ryman Auditorium stage since 1943 and transferred to the new Opry House when it opened in 1974. I dared not think of the celebrated artists with names such as Cash, Pride, Waylon, Willie, Reba, Garth, or Trisha who had stood on those same floorboards.

Brent kicked off "Break Down Here" with his signature guitar intro, and suddenly I was singing to nearly four thousand people in the Opry House and millions more on the coast-to-coast WSM radio broadcast. I glanced back at Brent and caught his smile that let me know I was doing okay. My confidence soared, and I stepped out of the circle and made my way to each side of the stage as I sang so I could interact more easily with the people in the crowd witnessing my Opry debut. The audience responded enthusiastically, some even singing along with me on the last chorus as I moved back to center stage. I ended the song where I had started it, right in the center of the circle.

For the first time, I allowed myself to think, *Patsy Cline used to stand here and sing!*

As I walked offstage, I waved at the crowd and said, "Thank you so much for having me tonight. This is a dream come true!"

The record company pitched my sound as "a blend of country and blues that embraces country's heritage while embarking on fresh, new, contemporary musical paths"—and finally, I broke through. I don't know whether it was attributable to my appearance on the Grand Ole Opry, or the many stops on the radio tour, or the cumulative efforts of Jason's media team, but "Break Down Here" landed on the Billboard chart. It first showed up at number thirty-five, then the song shot up to number sixteen. The video for "Break Down Here" debuted at the number-one spot on CMT.

Our radio tour culminated on May 25, 2004, at a CD release party sponsored by WSOC-FM radio at the Carolina Place Mall in Charlotte, North Carolina. Not only was this the first time I would perform near my hometown area since becoming a Mercury recording artist, but it was also the first time I would see my CD, simply titled *Julie Roberts*, on the record store shelves. I was super excited! I saw posters of me all over the store, and everywhere I looked, I saw myself looking back at me from another shelf. The thrill of seeing row after row of my CDs was more than I ever imagined it would be.

I chose a green silk top and white pants and speckled high heels for this appearance. I wasn't sure if many people would show up for this event, but I sure hoped so, and I wanted to look and sound my best for them.

As I walked through one of the mall's long service hallways on my way to the stage at the center court of the mall, I could hear a faint, "Julie, Julie!" The closer I got to the doorway leading to the stage, the louder the sound: "Julie! *Julie! JULIE!*

I heard the deejay, Jeff Roper, announce me as I stepped through the door, and I almost cried. On all sides of me, the mall was packed with people, and they were calling out my name—"Julie! JULIE!" It was amazing! It was as though I was attending my own pep rally, and everyone was rooting for me.

I sang some of the songs from my new album and thanked the Carolinians for coming out to the event. I think I thanked them about a dozen times that day, but it was really a special moment for me.

Following my set, I waved and said, "I hope I'm doing y'all proud!" and the crowd responded with a roar of applause and cheers.

The PR team whisked me away to the store where I saw an entire wall of CDs with my photo on them. It was emotionally overwhelming, but I signed CDs and photos for every person who was in line, and when the last person left, I was still on cloud nine.

It had happened! The dream had come true. Not only

was I now officially a Mercury recording artist, but hundreds of people had purchased my music!

Luke quipped, "She's made a brilliant record, and as long as the record company doesn't mess it up, we'll have success."

9

Welcome to the Whirlwind

One late night a few months later, Cory and I were sitting on the couch in the living room at the townhouse where Mama and I lived when he brought up an idea that shocked me.

"Hey, let's get married," he said, almost as nonchalantly as suggesting that we go out for sushi.

"What?" I responded. My eyes widened in surprise and confused thoughts raced through my mind. "What are you talking about?"

"You know, like the two of us as husband and wife."

"Okay," I said. Silently, I finished the statement: *Why not?*

Cory gave me a beautiful diamond ring that night. I

knew we were great friends, shared a love for music, and were both ambitious, yet there was a chemistry missing that I felt was necessary for marriage. I knew it wasn't right, but I didn't want to hurt him, so I said yes mainly because I did not know how to say no. Cory was such a nice guy, and he had been so helpful to me. After all, he was the person who had unselfishly introduced me to Brent, who had taken my music to Luke, who had . . . well, you get the idea. So I said, "Yes, I will marry you."

A few months after Cory and I got engaged, Mama and I were talking casually in the kitchen when she surprised me by asking, "Julie, are you sure you are in love with Cory?" I knew that Mama loved Cory and appreciated him for all that he had done for me. I knew she was not speaking negatively about my fiancé.

"Yes, Mama," I said. "Of course I am." I wasn't lying; I believed what I was saying because I *wanted* to be in love.

Mama looked me in the eyes. "I don't think you are," she said.

"Mama! How can you say that? We've been together for more than two years. Isn't that long enough to know that what we have is real? We're going to get married."

"Okay, you do what you want," Mama said, "but I don't think you love him." We dropped the subject, but I couldn't get Mama's comment out of my mind.

Cory's family, on the other hand, was marvelously supportive, and before long, his mom started sending bridal magazines to me. When I saw the magazines, it hit me that this was real—and I knew I couldn't go through with it.

Cory was ready to get married; he had his whole life

planned—job, home, car, two kids, the whole package . . . and I didn't. My career was just beginning.

"I can't do this," I finally told him. "I don't have my life planned out like you do. Not that I don't want to get married someday, but I'm not ready now. I think there's somebody else out there for you."

Cory was devastated at first, but he slowly came to the realization that I was right. I gave him back the beautiful ring, and we broke up but remained friends. He left the music business and pursued a master's degree in business. Cory went on to marry a fabulous woman; they have a couple of great kids, and Cory became a highly respected executive in the health-care industry—all just as he had planned.

Although I was finished with Mercury's boot camp, I still wanted to maintain a strict regimen of diet and exercise. I've always been a stress eater, and I knew I had to work hard to maintain the progress I had achieved. Even now, when I have a bad day, I find the almond butter! When things are going well, and I am working out regularly, my weight stays under control. But when life's tensions rise, weight gain is the inevitable result for me. I tend to medicate with food. So I was running on a treadmill at a Bellevue gym, not far from my home, and listening to WKDF-FM radio in Nashville when I heard a familiar song. Eddie Foxx, the morning-show deejay, was playing "Break Down Here."

I could hardly believe it! I had heard my music on the radio every day when I had been out on the radio promotions

tour. But this was the first time I'd heard my song on a normal day, doing normal things, hearing it just the random way
anyone else would.

I was so excited I nearly fell off the treadmill. I barely
restrained myself from shouting, "Hey, everybody, listen!
That's me on the radio!"

Things were happening so rapidly I could hardly keep
up with them. I wasn't scared, because I'd always dreamed
of being backstage and hearing the crowd out front. Now,
it was happening. Nevertheless, the reality was a heady
experience.

The flurry of media and magazine interviews continued
once my album came out in May 2004. The CMT hour-long
documentary *In the Moment* aired the first week of June,
and the *Glamour, Ladies' Home Journal*, and *People* magazine
features stirred up a lot of attention as well. In describing
my look and sound, *People* said, "She looks like Faith Hill
and sounds like Bonnie Raitt, which makes for a winning
combination for Julie Roberts." I thought that was quite a
nice compliment!

Looking back, even with a degree in music business and
several years' experience working at a major record label, I'm
not sure I truly understood what a blessing it was to have
all these talented people working on my behalf. They not
only knew how to make things happen, but they also had the
clout to get things done. Universal ran my fan club, letting
people know when and where I was playing, so I never had
to worry about whether people would show up.

Shortly after I returned to Nashville following the debut
of my album, the label arranged my first appearance during

CMA Fest, the weeklong celebration of country music held in early June that annually draws hundreds of thousands of fans to Nashville. The label planned a fan-club show where they introduced new artists, Josh Turner and me, at the party, and from there it seemed I went nonstop, from one event to another.

Creative Artists Agency had booked me at music festivals across the country that summer and finally booked my first paid solo gig, in Port St. Joe, Florida. Standing backstage by myself, waiting to go on, my body tingled with excitement as I heard the emcee say, *"Entertainment Weekly* awarded her self-titled CD an A rating, heralding it as 'one of the most auspicious debuts in years.' The *New York Times* described Julie's 'aching and resolute' hit 'Break Down Here' as 'one of the year's best country ballads.' Country Music Television recently featured Julie as the first artist ever to appear in the network's hour-long documentary *In the Moment,* and *USA Today* says that Julie is the female artist to watch out for!"

As the announcer's voice intensified, I could feel the butterflies fluttering in my stomach. But I was smiling, too, because I was so happy to finally be playing for a promoter who knew my music and liked it enough to choose me from among the myriad country music artists. *Okay, they are setting me up,* I thought. *These people believe in me, so I'm going to go out there and play a great show for them.*

And then came my favorite part of all . . . "Please welcome Mercury recording artist Julie Roberts!" That first performance, and every one after it, was an exhilarating experience for me.

On August 30, the nominations were announced simultaneously in Nashville and New York for the 2004 Country Music Awards to be presented at the Grand Ole Opry during a live November 9 broadcast on CBS. I was too nervous to listen. I knew the nominations were scheduled to be announced that morning, so I purposely tried to sleep in. *Will I be nominated or excluded?* I fretted. I was still in bed when shortly after eight o'clock, my phone rang. I was reluctant to pick it up, but I saw that it was Ron Shapiro calling. "Julie, this is Ron and Jason Owen," Ron gushed exuberantly. "Guess whaaaat?"

"What?" I deadpanned.

"You are nominated for your first CMA Award!"

I leaped out of bed. "Are you sure?"

"We're sure!" Jason Owen chimed in. "Congratulations." Jason immediately went into PR mode, instructing me about how I should answer media requests. Ron slowed him down a bit by reading the list of the other nominees to me over the phone. And there was my name, nominated for the Horizon Award (which would be renamed the New Artist of the Year Award)—right alongside Dierks Bentley; Big & Rich; Josh Turner, who was riding his hit song, "Long Black Train"; and Gretchen Wilson, who was flying high following the success of her number-one hit, "Redneck Woman." Even more exciting, I was invited to sing "Break Down Here" during the telecast, which would be viewed by millions of people around the world!

In the meantime, my agents booked me as part of the 2004 Rascal Flatts "Here's to You" concert tour, appearing in arenas in twenty-eight cities beginning in September. I didn't know the guys well, but I knew they were hot and on a roll, packing arenas across the country. I would be the opening act on the show along with Capitol Records artist Chris Cagle, who had already scored a couple of top ten hits.

The deal was not good for me in some ways and great in others. A dirty little secret in the music business is that on most tours, the opening acts are not paid (so be especially nice to them when you attend concerts). In many cases, the record company or artist management actually has to *pay* the headliner for a new artist to be included on the show.

That was the situation when I went out on tour with Rascal Flatts. "The label will pay for your bus and your band, and normal travel per diems," my manager, Ron, informed me. "You won't be getting paid, but you can sell merchandise at each concert. And you can sign autographs at the end of the show, but not before the Rascal Flatts set is over."

I was ecstatic to be performing on such a significant tour, even though I would not be earning any money. The good news was that all my expenses would be covered by Mercury. The bad news was that all the expenses—the tour bus, the band, luxurious hotels, food, everything that the record company was paying for—were added to the balance I owed the label.

My account with the label was already astronomically in debt due to the radio tour. Although I did not have to repay the company out of my pocket, any money that came in, whether through sales of albums, T-shirts, pictures, or fan-club memberships, was levied against the huge amount that had to be recouped before I would actually make a profit. That wasn't unusual. That's just the way the music business works.

On tour with Rascal Flatts, I was in awe the first time I played in one of the huge arenas. We played to packed houses and sold-out crowds everywhere we went. Each night, I opened the show; then Chris did the middle set, followed by Rascal Flatts. At the conclusion of the show, I joined the other artists onstage for an encore. Then I'd hurry out to my table to greet the fans and sign autographs. I enjoyed meeting the fans, and of course, merchandise sales helped people to become more familiar with my music.

Most tour dates usually began the night before for me, when I met my bus in the Kroger parking lot near my home. Even in Nashville, where tour buses are common sights, people don't really appreciate a big bus pulling into a neighborhood in the middle of the night, so most artists and bands meet at a convenient central location. For me, that was the grocery store parking lot closest to my home. Normally, I showed up at midnight with my pajamas, ready to go to bed, but the guys in the band almost always wanted to grab some last-minute snacks from the grocery store, so I'd wear something casual so I could go snack shopping with them in the wee hours.

By one o'clock in the morning, we were rolling, with posted times for arrival, sound check, backstage catering, and any special preshow activities. Ordinarily, I would get up early to exercise and to do any available radio interviews in whatever city in which we were performing. By the time

I got back, it would be almost time for sound check. Then it was time to clean up and get ready for the show. It was always a thrill for me to see my name on the dressing room door.

The opening act was allotted a maximum of thirty minutes. I was informed emphatically by the tour manager, "*Never* exceed your allotted time onstage. No matter how well the audience responds, or how much you want to give them a little something extra, you gotta make it happen within your thirty minutes. Do not run over time." The manager also was very strict about how loud my concert performance could be. The Flatts's sound guy met with my bandleader and my sound engineer and told them not to exceed so many decibels.

One of the rules of being the opening act, I quickly learned, was that "it's not about you." Everything always had to be bigger and better for the headliner, in this case, Rascal Flatts. That meant more lights, louder sound, better staging; it was their show, and nothing was ever to take the attention away from them.

Each night, I opened the show, sang my heart out, and hopefully left the audience wanting more. The look my record label wanted me to present was "classy country casual." I usually wore expensive, ripped jeans—provided by my record label's PR department—with high heels and a cute top, but I did not wear dresses for the Rascal Flatts shows. They dressed casually onstage, so that set the tone for Chris and me as well.

Occasionally, my record label representatives or the tour manager asked me to wear something special for the finale. For instance, when the tour played Knoxville, my record label wanted to hype the impression that I was dating a star athlete from the University of Tennessee, so they had me wear a jersey with his number for the show's finale. It was totally contrived publicity. I didn't even know the guy, much less had I ever dated him.

"This will win over the local radio guys," I was told. I wore the jersey, and sure enough, the local station played my record—a lot!

At the close of the show each night, both Chris Cagle and I returned to the stage for the show's encore and finale. By then the crowd was almost ecstatic, and the arena was rocking. The Flatts show included a ramp that extended out into the audience, and we all made our way out onto the ramp, as each of us sang our solo lines, as well as the group parts, slapping hands with the audience members at the front of the stage.

Each night, after the show, we had what the tour manager referred to as the "Flatts Shack," a special room where the road managers had invited fans to join the artists and bands for a postshow party. I didn't know who decided on the guest list or what the criteria was for someone to be invited, but I noticed after the first or second date that there were no unattractive people in the Flatts Shack. It was sort of an extended meet and greet, complete with food and drink—lots of drink.

By the end of each concert day, I was dead tired and not really in the mood for partying. "Do you really think I need to go to the Flatts Shack every night?" I asked my manager.

"It's a relationship business, Julie," Ron said. "We're hoping that you can establish great relationships with everyone so you will be high on their list for the next tour. If you stay to yourself, nobody will get to know you. I think it would be good for you to attend the aftershow parties."

He had a point. "Okay, Ron. If you think I should." So I attended as often as I could.

Then every night, I'd return to the back bedroom of the bus to enjoy my own postshow ritual: a viewing of the movie about Patsy Cline's life, *Sweet Dreams*. I loved Patsy Cline, and I loved the movie, so I would go to sleep with *Sweet Dreams* on my mind.

On November 9, 2004, I attended the Country Music Association's award show in Nashville. My label flew in a celebrity hair and makeup artist from Los Angeles for the event. Early in the afternoon, a limousine driver picked me up at home and took me to the hotel, where my wardrobe awaited me in the makeup artist's suite. Wardrobe personnel flitted in and out of the room. I chewed my usual Trident sugarless gum to help stay calm, as more and more people came into the room, checking on our progress, making sure that I would be on time for my first-ever red-carpet appearance. All the while, Jason Owen coached me regarding how I could best respond to interview questions thrown at me on the red carpet.

"Be sure that you are not chewing gum when you walk the carpet," he instructed. I appreciated his advice, but he was making me even more nervous.

I wore a long, green, satin fitted dress for the event. Jason checked me over from head to toe, again and again, before I left the hotel room to head to the Grand Ole Opry House.

The chauffeur dropped me off right at the beginning of the red carpet. Throngs of fans crowded against the ropes on both sides as I followed Jason up the carpet, with Jason fielding interview requests from media and me pausing briefly to talk with every interviewer who had a microphone or a camera. Jason guided me to particular media outlets that he wanted to make sure I talked with before going inside. I stopped repeatedly to take photos with fans along the line. It was exhilarating and intimidating at the same time. Camera flashes blinded me, and people called out to me from every direction. All the reporters wanted to know, "Who are you wearing?" I didn't know designer names well enough to let them roll off my tongue, so Jason had written them down on a card and put it inside my purse, designed by someone else I didn't know.

My favorite part of the preshow activities was standing in front of the "step and repeat" CMA backdrop where photographers begged for me to step first in one direction then another, then repeat that pose over and over, as they snapped their photos.

Because I was performing on the show, I had access to a backstage dressing room that I shared with Faith Hill and Martina McBride. I met Mama there, and we did final touch-ups before we were escorted to our seats.

We sat next to Vince Gill and his wife, Amy Grant. "Hey, kiddo," Vince said when he saw me. "Good luck."

It is almost expected at award shows to say something self-effacing such as, "I'm honored simply to be nominated," and I repeated that statement a lot that night. And I really *did* feel honored to be nominated, but it was still awkward to sit in the front of the Opry House with the television cameras trained on me as the winner of the Horizon Award was announced. I could feel my body tense as LeAnn Rimes and Joe Nichols stood at the microphone and said, "And the 2004 Horizon Award goes to . . . Gretchen Wilson!"

The Opry House erupted in applause, as it seemed that more than four thousand people rose to their feet simultaneously in recognition of Gretchen's outstanding achievements. I'd had a great start to my career, and my album was selling fantastically, but Gretchen Wilson had enjoyed a phenomenal year. It was only right that she won the Horizon Award. I was happy for her. Still, it hurt just a little that I had not won.

I was excited when the Rascal Flatts tour swept through the Carolinas in early November. As always, radio station WSOC-FM rolled out the red carpet for us and promoted the concert big-time, and we had a fantastic, enthusiastic crowd for the show.

Universal rented the Sunset Club, a private facility in Charlotte, to host a Listener Appreciation Show, a special auxiliary concert for the winners of a WSOC-FM-sponsored contest. Because we were so close to my hometown, I invited my sister Marie and her husband, Jimmy, to attend the event and to bring their newborn baby. I was especially excited to meet my first niece, Torie Rebecca, who had been born the previous month.

At the event, Mickey Cones, my guitar player, and I performed a few songs acoustically and then circulated throughout the crowd. After I'd greeted as many people as possible, I went into a side room where Marie, Jimmy, and baby Torie were waiting for me.

Along with them and a few other people were two large, good-looking guys. E. J., my label's radio rep, had mentioned that a few NFL players would be in attendance, and I spotted them right away. I often watched football while traveling on the bus. I enjoyed the games, but even more often, I'd point out one of the players and tell E. J., "Ooo, he's so cute!"

Marie told me the players' names were Eric and Jack. She had been talking with them earlier and was more in awe that she had been able to talk with the professional football players than she was that I was being featured as an artist.

I was excited too. I had never been to an NFL game at that point in my life, and I'd certainly never met one of the players.

"Well, introduce me." I nudged Marie. "I want to meet them!"

Both were handsome and seemed to be in excellent physical shape. Eric seemed more my type, but Marie was more taken with Jack. "He seems like a really genuine person. He was asking me all about Torie. How many football players want to talk about a baby? I think he is really nice."

"No, I think Eric is cuter," I said, flashing a big smile in his direction.

Acting as though she and the players were best buddies, Marie introduced me to Jack and Eric. Eric was soon drawn away to speak to someone else, however, so Jack and I struck up a conversation.

"I'm sorry I didn't recognize you," he said politely. "I don't really listen to country music. That's more of Eric's thing. He's a huge country music fan. Eric knows your music. He heard that you were coming, so I'm really here with him."

Strike two for Jack; two points for Eric, I thought.

Jack and I chatted further, but I kept my eye on Eric throughout the conversation. At the close of the evening, Jack asked for my phone number, and like a giddy schoolgirl, I gave it to him.

That night our group stayed at a hotel in Charlotte. I called Marie and gave her the full report, including the fact that Jack had no idea who I was.

"I think it is good that he didn't know anything about you or what you do," Marie said. "Maybe he likes you for who you are."

"Okay, maybe you're right." I wanted to believe that my sister recognized something potentially great that I didn't see.

I hung up with Marie and started to get ready for bed. I looked up, and to my surprise, I saw a number of ladybugs on the ceiling. For some reason, I've always considered ladybugs a positive sign.

I called Marie again and said, "Marie, I think it is a sign. My hotel room is infatuated with ladybugs."

"*Infatuated?*" Marie said with a laugh. "Don't you mean *infested?*"

"No, *infatuated!*" I said. "I think that I was supposed to meet Jack, and the ladybugs are a sign that this is going to be the start of something great."

Marie wasn't convinced, but I think I convinced myself. I could not have been more wrong.

Early the next morning, I was aboard a plane on my way to Oregon when Jack called. He left a message on my voice mail, asking if we could get together over Thanksgiving, and that began a long-distance phone relationship. Before long, I was crazy about the friendly football player, even if he wasn't a fan of country music.

It had already been announced that the 2005 CMA Awards show was going to be held in New York City instead of its usual home in Nashville. To capitalize on the publicity, the CMA flew Mama, Marie, and me to New York on a private jet so I could appear in the Macy's Thanksgiving Day Parade and ride on the CMA float promoting the 2005 awards. It was my first time to fly aboard a private jet, and Mama, Marie, and I looked around the plane in awe. The CMA also brought along a makeup artist, as well as several CMA executives.

In addition to waving and smiling along the parade route, I was scheduled to perform one song during the annual Macy's Thanksgiving Day Parade, broadcast live to millions of people. As a child, I had watched the parade every Thanksgiving along with my sisters, while Mama cooked up a feast. Now, here I was, standing alone on my float amid the cheerful chaos, while Mama and Marie were watching the parade and eating chocolate with Ron Shapiro in Macy's greenroom.

I didn't realize prior to this that the singers in the parade were not really singing but were lip-synching—I'd be singing along to a full-blown soundtrack that included my vocals. It was the first time I ever lip-synched anywhere, much less on live television seen all over the country. I was to perform "Ain't Down Home," a song from my album, and I had to do it exactly as I had sung it in the studio, something I had never even done in my live performances. I practiced in front of a mirror in my hotel room to make sure my words matched the recording.

Bundled up in a cute, formfitting winter outfit, I rode on the float and waved to the thousands of people lining the streets. When we got to the judges' stand, the float stopped and the emcee announced me. I "sang" my song and finished out the parade waving and smiling my way through the streets of New York City. It was so much fun!

Following the parade, we headed straight to the airport and boarded the CMA plane back to Charlotte, so we could try to get home for Thanksgiving dinner.

The plane was stocked with all sorts of snacks and four-hundred-dollar-per-bottle Cristal champagne. Marie abstained from alcohol, but Mama and I did not. We had never tasted such expensive champagne in our lives. I planned to meet Jack and some of his friends for dinner once we got back to Charlotte, so the CMA makeup artist reapplied my makeup and did my nails. I felt like a queen.

A short time after takeoff, we hit turbulence. The plane bounced and jerked violently, sending candy dishes flying in every direction.

Most of us on the plane were laughing—probably due

to the champagne—but Marie was absolutely freaking out. "I have a new baby and I'm fixin' to die!" she squalled.

Finally, Mama, in her usual direct manner, leaned over and confronted my sister. "Marie, quit your crying," she said. "When it's your time to go, you need to just put your head between your legs and kiss your butt goodbye! There's nothing you can do about it."

I laughed so hard, I forgot all about the turbulence. Funny, I remember that moment even more than the parade itself!

We made it through the rough weather and on to Charlotte, arriving home in time for a late Thanksgiving Day dinner. I thought, *Wow! That is the way to travel!*

The Rascal Flatts tour extended into the winter months all the way through the Christmas season. It was bitter cold the night the tour played Minneapolis. After the show, I went back to the Flatts Shack party, as usual.

I sipped one glass of wine as I talked and laughed with the band members and the special invited guests. Suddenly, the room began to swirl and I felt sick. I excused myself and walked back to my bus by myself.

My tour manager met me at the door of the bus as I stumbled up the steps and down the hall toward my bedroom. "Are you okay?" he asked.

"No, I feel like I'm in a disco," I told him. "Everything is really loud." The lights were on in the front lounge area of the bus, and it seemed as though the bus itself was swirling.

"You're back on the bus, and you're safe here," he said. "Why don't you try to get some rest?"

I crawled into bed and didn't wake up until the next morning.

When I saw my tour manager, I asked, "What happened last night?"

"I don't know," he said. "You looked pretty rough when you came in. Do you remember how much you had to drink?"

"Only one glass," I said, "that someone handed to me when I walked in."

After I described to him the order of events at the Flatts Shack, he said, "Julie, I've seen this before. I think somebody slipped something into your drink."

"Really? Oh my gosh. I'm never going back in there again."

"Have you ever reacted that way to wine before?"

"No, never." I felt afraid, horrified that my trust had been violated.

The next day, I went to the Mall of America to buy Christmas gifts for my family. As I walked around the mall, I thought about what had happened. I realized that I was too naive and trusting and that I needed to grow up. Although I was the lone woman on the tour, I never imagined that someone might try to take advantage of me, especially with all my band buddies surrounding me. But the incident was a wake-up call for me. Even though I felt like I was flying high, I realized that I needed to be more cautious and more aware of the potential dangers of success in the music business.

Following the tour, I felt like a family member with the guys from Rascal Flatts, their band and crew, as well as Chris Cagle. Whenever we saw each other at music industry events or awards shows, it was fun to reminisce. It was great to interact with my new friends, and even more heartwarming to realize that they now regarded me as a peer.

10

Striking Gold!

I was back home in Nashville, trying to recuperate from the holiday season and the several months of consistent touring, when I received a call from Erin, my replacement in Luke's office.

"Mr. Lewis . . . er, I mean, Luke wants to see you right away, Julie," Erin said. Her voice sounded almost mysterious, as though she were planning a surprise birthday party, but my birthday was still a few weeks away.

"Okay, Erin," I said. "I'll be right over. What's this all about?"

"I'm not really sure," she said. "Sounds important, though. He wants to talk with you in person."

"All right. I just finished working out. I'll get there as soon as I can."

I took a quick shower, threw on my clothes and makeup, and drove downtown to the Universal Music Group offices. Once inside, I quickly made my way to Luke's private office suite. I smiled as I remembered the many mornings I'd hurried to arrive at those offices before the record label heads, just so I could get their coffee ready or prepare their morning schedules. Now *my* name was on Luke's schedule.

I arrived outside Luke's office, a little out of breath from rushing, and smiled openly when I saw Erin sitting at the desk, guarding Luke's door.

"Sorry it took so long," I said. "Is he ready for me?" I posed in front of her desk, modeling the new outfit Jason Owen had recommended I wear for industry events.

Erin looked up and raised her eyebrows, nodding admiringly. "Oh yeah. He's ready for you," she said with a laugh. "You better get right in there." Erin motioned me toward Luke's office door, smiling at me as she got up and whispered, "Hard to believe that just a little more than a year ago. . . ." She glanced back at her desk, but she didn't need to finish her statement.

Erin opened the door for me, and I stepped in Luke's office. I was momentarily stunned as the room erupted in loud cheers and applause from Luke, Jason Owen, Brent Rowan, and a half dozen or more Mercury and Universal record executives, some of whose names I didn't even know. My mouth dropped open, and I looked at the group with startled confusion on my face. This was clearly not an ordinary meeting.

"What's goin' on?" I asked. "Y'all wanna tell me what this is all about?"

Luke rose from behind his desk and crossed the room to where I was still standing near the door. He hugged me like a father and said, "You must be the only person in Nashville who doesn't know."

"Know? Know what?"

Luke didn't answer but instead reached for the latest edition of a report from the Record Industry Association of America, the official certifying organization that tracks the sales of albums in all genres of music, not only country music.

I looked at the report and saw my name and my album highlighted under the section signifying sales of more than a half-million albums.

Luke smiled at me broadly. "It's *gold*, Julie!" he said. "Your album just became a gold record, with sales of more than five hundred thousand albums, and it is still going!"

"Yeessss!" I shrieked with joy. "Oh, thank you, Luke. This is fantastic!"

"Better yet, the spin count from radio is going through the roof," he said. "Not just on 'Break Down Here,' but other cuts from the album as well. We've gotta work hard to make sure that holds. Jason's already lining up some good media." Luke looked toward Jason.

"I've expanded the media tour to broaden your market base," Jason said, "plus I'm lining up some major TV appearances to help promote the album and get the public anticipating the next one. I've been on the phone already today with the Leno people."

"The Leno people?" I asked.

"Yeah, as in Jay Leno." Jason smiled. "As in the *Tonight Show*. They want you on as soon as possible, so we're going to make that happen. We have a feature in *Vanity Fair*, and I have a few other surprises cooked up as well."

"Thank you, Jason!" I said. "You are amazing."

Brent had quietly sidled over next to me. He looked me in the eyes and said, "I told you, 'I believe it,' and this just goes to show that other people do too. Congratulations, Julie." He hugged me and smiled.

"Oh, Brent, I couldn't have done it without you!" I gushed.

"Sure, you could have," he said. "You're the singer. I just twist the knobs on the recording console."

"Yeah, well, you twist them all in the right directions," I said and hugged him again.

"I've already started collecting songs we can review for the next album," Brent said.

"The next album?" I said. "Can't I just enjoy this a little bit first?"

Brent smiled. "Sure, you can. For a few days." He smiled again, but I could tell he was serious. "One thing you need to know about this business, Julie. Having a hit album is not enough. You've got to keep on having them. Your next album will be just as important as your first. Maybe more so."

"I know," I said, looking at Brent and speaking quietly so Luke and Jason couldn't hear. "Nashville's full of one-hit wonders. But I'm not gonna be one of them. Thanks to you."

"Ha," Brent laughed. "No, you're here to stay, and it won't be long till you leave me in your dust. You've got me on this album, but you'll be looking around for someone else to produce you soon."

"No way," I replied with a laugh. "Don't even say such a thing. You're my producer, and I want it to stay that way."

Brent shrugged. "We'll see," he said.

Luke interrupted our conversation. "I've arranged a little party in your honor, Julie. When is that date, Jason?"

Jason looked at his phone and quickly found the information. "Wednesday, February second, at the Mirror restaurant downtown. Can you make that, Julie?"

"I . . . well, I think . . . I guess so," I joked. "Yeesss!"

"Everybody who's anybody in the Nashville music industry here in town will be there, and some out-of-town guests as well. We'll have plenty to eat and drink and lots of good PR ops. I'm already working on TV coverage."

Jason hugged me and said, "Congratulations, Julie. It has a nice ring to it, doesn't it? Julie goes gold!"

The "gold" party was another dream come true for me. Not even the cold February temperatures or the soaking drizzle in the night air could dim my spirits as I stepped through the back entrance of the Mirror, an upscale Nashville restaurant. My only disappointment was that Mama had to work late and wouldn't be able to arrive until the festivities were well underway.

"Don't you worry," she had said. "I'll get there. I wouldn't miss this party for anything!"

Of course, Jason Owen selected my outfit, the high heels

the label wanted me to wear to reinforce my image, and even my hairstyle. Jason designed everything I did—including the gold-record celebration—as a vehicle for more publicity. He was an expert at not only managing PR but creating it.

True to the establishment's name, the restaurant décor featured mirrors everywhere, all reflecting gold—gold candles flickering throughout the room, gold napkins, and gold-lined dishes and wineglasses. Even the chocolate fountain in the center of the room was decked out with "gold." Guests flitted around the room, embracing one another, munching hors d'oeuvres, and making industry small talk. Just as Jason had predicted, the room was crowded with music industry movers and shakers. There were not many other artists, although there were a few, such as Joe Nichols, celebrating with me. The success of Joe's album, produced by Brent Rowan, had been a milestone in his career and in Brent's as well. Brent seemed to be enjoying the attention as he mingled in the crowd, accepting well-deserved congratulations for his production skills.

Joining Luke Lewis and his staff was James Stroud from Universal Music Group, the parent company of my label, Mercury Records. Pete Fisher, who had expertly managed the Grand Ole Opry for years and practically single-handedly decided who appeared on that famous stage, hobnobbed with label heads and PR people seeking his attention. Representatives from the Country Music Association were there as well.

I moved from one camera to another, guided by Jason Owen, with a special makeup artist provided by the label dabbing powder on my beaming face before each interview. I couldn't keep from smiling. Nor did I try!

After about an hour of meeting and greeting, James Stroud stood on the restaurant's improvised stage and opened the formal part of the ceremonies. Calling me to the stage, James said, "Ladies and gentlemen, the greatest smile in music, Julie Roberts!" I stepped up onto the stage with the music mogul, both of us smiling broadly.

"A gold record—signifying the sales of more than five hundred thousand albums—is increasingly hard to come by," James said, glancing at me and then at the crowd. He turned again to me. "It's a huge night for you, Julie, and a huge night for us."

James introduced Rick Murray, the Country Music Association's senior director of strategic marketing, who presented me with a certificate of achievement celebrating the gold record. Handing me the certificate, Rick said to the audience, "Julie Roberts truly is America's sweetheart!"

Luke Lewis retold the inside story of me having worked in his office as his assistant. He then assured the guests and well-wishers that my album had reached the gold level on its own merit. "As good as we are at the record company over there," he said, nodding toward Music Row, "this wasn't a bag of tricks."

I looked at Luke appreciatively. "I hope you have a big wall, Julie," he said. He picked up the large gold-record plaque. "Because this is just the first one. I can't tell you how proud I am of you."

Tears welled in my eyes at Luke's spontaneous expression of approval. I struggled to keep from crying. The crowded room seemed to reverberate with applause and cheers as Luke presented to me the framed gold-record plaque.

By then Mama had arrived and was standing at the back of the room.

"Mama, look!" I exclaimed as I took the large plaque from Luke's hands. I thanked Luke for his willingness to take a chance on me, and then looked at Brent, who was standing near the front.

"I really am indebted to Brent Rowan," I said. "Besides being a musical genius, Brent was the first man who believed in me and didn't tell me that I should find another career." The audience laughed but also nodded in understanding at Brent's key role in my success.

I then turned my attention toward Mama, who I could tell even from a distance was already crying. I looked out at the crowd and said, "My 'other half' is here tonight," nodding toward Mama. "Mama got here late from working at the factory. She's given me every penny she's ever had to help me get this gold record." I held the album plaque up a little higher as I waved Mama to the stage. The crowd applauded the woman most responsible for my success. I handed the gold-record plaque to Mama. It was the first time in my life that I felt I had tangible evidence honoring the sacrifices she had made for me. Mama and I hugged onstage, and I said, "You get one of these, too, Mama!"

It was a powerfully emotional evening. I had attended similar parties for other artists. Now I couldn't help thinking, *All of this is for me?* It was one of those nights I had dreamed of since childhood, and I didn't want it to end. But I knew that Brent was right—it was time to get back to work. We had to come up with a second album, and it had to be great—or else.

11

Song-Stress

I was excited to get back into the recording studio with Brent Rowan, searching for songs and crafting a follow-up album to my first release, *Julie Roberts*. The process was more structured than our previous sessions because I was also traveling on tour throughout the country, performing concerts. Even finding the songs took longer because I was committed to finding songs I could connect with. For me the best songs are always the ones I can imagine myself experiencing, living vicariously through the lyrics.

Since I now had a record deal, songwriters and publishers pitched songs to Brent and me constantly. I also had my own music publishing deal, so I could now write my own songs, but there was no guarantee that the label would accept them for my album.

Luke Lewis emphasized to Brent how important it was that my second album be better than my first, that it had to work for radio, so Brent pulled in some outside musicians to help, including prominent LA studio drummer Vinnie Colaiuta, who had played on Faith Hill's smash albums.

Brent and I wanted to record in a similar fashion as we had done my first album, with just the two of us in the studio, especially as I was singing my vocals. But the label was in a hurry for us to get the second album done. They wanted to hear something right away. We weren't really ready for that, as Brent and I had experienced some microphone problems early on in the studio that slowed us down. Brent requested and received new microphones, and we started all over again.

Luke was insistent that he wanted to hear some of our recordings, so Brent reluctantly sent him a cut of the first song we had recorded. Shortly after that, Luke called me to his office. He was obviously displeased with what he had heard, even though he knew we'd been having microphone problems.

"I don't think you've hooked this with Brent," Luke said flatly. "It's a hit song, but you haven't recorded a hit. I know you've been having microphone problems, but I think I want to make a change."

"What sort of change?" I expected Luke to say that we were switching studios or calling in musicians who had worked with us previously. I was totally unprepared for Luke's response.

"I want to bring in a new producer," Luke said. "I want you to work with Byron Gallimore."

I was familiar with Byron, but didn't really know him. I knew he had recently produced Lee Ann Womack's hit album that had earned Album of the Year accolades, and I loved the results they had achieved. But I was concerned about my friend.

"What about Brent?" I asked.

"Brent won't be finishing the album with you, Julie," Luke said. "You're getting a whole new team."

I was stunned and confused. "What do you mean 'Brent won't be finishing the album'? We've already started."

"You guys aren't getting what we need for this new record," Luke said.

"But we've got some great songs . . . some that I've helped write. They are personal and real to me. Isn't that what country music is all about?"

"Yes, you have some good songs." Luke nodded affirmatively. "But they're not good enough for your second album. Your first album went gold, so we are shooting for this one to go platinum. That means we need songs that are going to play on the radio. It's all about the number of spins."

I felt sick to my stomach. "Well, I need to talk to Brent," I said sadly. "I need to tell him what's going on."

"No," Luke said. "Brian Wright, head of A&R, will tell him."

I knew Brian, and he was a kind, quality person who had worked with Brent and me by going to song meetings in search of material for the album. I felt sure he would handle the situation delicately. I resigned myself to the fact that this change was inevitable, regardless of how much I protested.

"Okay, but I still want to talk to him," I said.

"No, that's not a good idea," Luke said emphatically. "You stay out of it." He implied that there were legalities and fiduciary issues involved in making such a change.

"I feel like I should at least call Brent. We've had a lot of success together. And we're friends."

"Julie," Luke said firmly. "Do not call Brent. Let Brian take care of it."

Unfortunately, the message got to Brent before Brian or anyone else from Mercury contacted him. Brent was playing guitar on a session for another artist, when somebody said, "Hey, I just did a session on Julie's record with Byron Gallimore. I thought you were producing the new Julie Roberts album."

"I thought I was too," Brent replied. That was the way he found out that he wasn't.

I did not know about that conversation at the time, nor did I know that Brent was unaware that he was off the project. It would be more than five years later that I learned that Brent thought I was the one who had requested a different producer. I was grieved that such a good, gentle-spirited man would be treated so callously.

Byron Gallimore, my new producer, immediately trashed all the previous work that Brent and I had recorded for my second album. Byron brought in an entirely new cast of players for my recording sessions. He oversaw new tracks, and we started over.

But when it came time for me to record my vocals, Byron rarely sat through a full recording session with me. He'd come into the studio in the morning, help us get organized and set the board, and then leave the actual recording work to his assistant. This was not at all the same working relationship I'd had with Brent, and that was disconcerting for me.

When Byron did sit in on sessions, he tried to expand my vocal range. On one song, I knew the note was too high for me. I worked on the song for quite a while with Byron's assistant, but standing out in the studio by myself, I confessed, "I don't think I can reach that note."

I heard Byron's voice on my headphones. "Don't worry. You can do it. Just go for it."

I appreciated Byron's encouragement, but I know my voice well. I know my range and where I am strongest. Under ordinary circumstances, I would have enjoyed attempting something new. But with Byron's new approach to recording combined with Luke's negative criticism, I had lost the confidence that I could do the impossible.

I sang the song, just as Byron asked and I hit the note he wanted me to reach but to me, it still did not sound right. I wanted to "hook it," whatever that meant, but I didn't feel that we were there yet.

"That's great," Byron said. "We can work with that."

"I can do it better," I protested.

"Oh no, that's fine," Byron said.

So I left it at that. I was confident that Byron knew what

he was doing. He was, after all, one of Nashville's premier producers. He knew what it took to create hit songs.

Maybe because of the bigger budget, loftier goals, and more pressure associated with my second album, Byron worked differently than Brent and I had done. After signing my recording deal, hardly anybody from Mercury heard my first album until Brent and I were completely done. But Byron wanted Luke's involvement during the process. When we finished a few cuts on the album, we turned them in to Luke so he could monitor our progress. I waited anxiously for his response.

From the time I left my job as Luke's assistant at Mercury, a few weeks after I received a recording deal, my only source of income was a small advance from Mercury and a publishing deal with EMI Music. Cory, my former fiancé, worked at EMI and was my first connection there, and my manager, Ron Shapiro, worked out the deal details for me. As part of the agreement, I was required to turn in to EMI a certain number of fully written songs per year. If I cowrote with another writer, that counted only as half of a song. In exchange, the publishing company paid me a monthly stipend. It wasn't a lot of money, but it was enough to pay my basic bills. Money was tight.

Interestingly, the publishers didn't want me to sing my own songs to demo for other artists, so the company hired outside singers to perform my songs. The company's rationale was that artists would not want to record my songs if they thought that I had passed on them for my own album. If the voice on the demo wasn't mine, that was one level of separation away from me, and the publishers found producers more willing to consider the songs.

Ben Vaughn, my publishing representative at EMI, told me John Rich wanted to write with me. That was great news—John had a reputation as one of Nashville's top songwriters, and his recent success as part of Big & Rich had catapulted him to even loftier heights. John had produced award-winning albums for Gretchen Wilson and Faith Hill, and he was riding high in the Nashville music community. He was also regarded as one of Nashville's more outrageous characters, notorious for wild parties at his home.

I knew John casually from meeting him at various industry events and award shows, but we weren't really friends. He was single, and to me he seemed wild as a buck at the time; he made me uneasy. I'd seen enough of that with my dad, and that was not the kind of person with whom I wanted to hang around, much less to write songs.

Nevertheless, Ron Shapiro, my manager, encouraged me to write with John. "Julie, everybody is paying attention to what John is writing," Ron said. "I think you need to do it." I trusted and loved my manager, but I still felt reluctant to write with somebody who reminded me so much of my dad. Ben Vaughn suggested that we add another female writer to the mix. That made sense to me.

"Okay, Ron, I'll do it," I said. "But only if we get another female writer to join us for the writing session."

So one summer morning, I got together with Victoria Vaughn, a successful songwriter in her own right, at John's house at ten o'clock in the morning. Since it was so warm, I dressed informally in shorts and a cute top. I greeted John and Victoria and we went upstairs to his studio area, where John had what looked like a soft-drink machine.

"Can I get you something to drink?" he asked, nodding toward the drink dispenser, which I now realized was loaded with whiskey. It was not yet noon, and John was already drinking.

"No, thanks," I said. "I'm good. I have a bottle of water with me."

We sat down and talked awhile, when John suddenly said, "I love your calves."

What? Did he really say that? Was he talking about me? Or is he already thinking about a song lyric? I had no idea. Maybe John was complimenting me, but the comment struck me as odd. Victoria didn't even seem to notice. Apparently, she knew John well, so not much surprised her.

It was an awkward start to a songwriting session. Nevertheless, we wrote a great song, "A Woman Knows," before we broke for lunch.

John wanted me to ride with him in his Corvette to the restaurant. I wasn't sure how much he'd had to drink, so everything within me said, *Don't get into that car.* But I did. I wanted to avoid an awkward scene or offending John. Victoria drove her own car. Smart girl. She had written and ridden with John before.

We sped through traffic, with John careening from lane to lane, barely veering away from oncoming vehicles at the last second. Although the restaurant was only a few miles away, it was one of the longest rides of my life! I was never so glad to reach a destination. I thought, *If Mama knew I was in a car with this dude, she would just die! Or kill me, one or the other.* After lunch, I made a hasty exit. I had to feed my dogs, pair my socks, anything! I just wanted to get away.

A few months later, Ben Vaughn called me. "John Rich is producing a new album on John Anderson, and John Anderson wants to record the song you and Victoria and John wrote."

That was the good news. The bad news was that because he was producing the album, John Rich wanted half of my publishing royalties for the song.

"I think you should do it," Ben suggested, "but it's your decision."

John may have felt that since he pitched the song to John Anderson and was producing the album, he deserved a higher percentage. But that arrangement didn't sound right to me. Royalties would already be split between three songwriters. Why did he think he was entitled to more of my portion?

Ben shrugged. "Well, everybody does it because they all want to be on a cut with John Rich."

This time, I stood my ground. "No, that's not acceptable to me."

"Are you sure?" Ben asked. "Nobody ever says no to John."

"I'm sure. If they don't want to cut the song, that's fine. But if they think it is worth recording, then the songwriter split should be equal between all three writers."

John never mentioned the awkward request to me, but I knew he was not happy.

John Anderson recorded the song, and to this day, John

Rich and I haven't written another song together. It was another life lesson about the subtle yet commonly understood maneuverings within Music City.

I didn't let the friction bother me. I was still working on new songs for my own album. And the anticipation among radio deejays, as well as the initial progress reports coming out of Luke's office, sounded promising.

12

Anxious Acquiescence

I had every reason to believe that my life and music career were moving in an upward direction, until that night my body betrayed me while on stage at the Orange Peel in Asheville. Prior to that experience, Mama and I had often joked, "We ain't skeered of nuttin'," but as I felt what seemed like an electric shock sear through my body from head to toe, I was more than scared. I was terrified. Strength fled from my hands, and I could not even hold the microphone.

What is going on? I screamed silently. *My fingertips can't feel anything. I can't see!* It was as though a dark haze had settled over my eyes, similar to what might happen when you step out of a brightly lit hallway into a dark movie theater. I kept waiting for my eyes to adjust, but they didn't.

Although my sense of touch returned after a while, my vision continued to be blurred throughout the remainder of the show. It was three or four hours later before I could see clearly again.

As soon as I got back to Nashville, I was examined by several doctors and underwent numerous tests at the hospital. I thought they were going to discover I had a brain tumor. *But they can operate on tumors, right?* I thought. *I'll be fine.*

I was shocked when my neurologist informed me that I had multiple sclerosis, a debilitating disease that normally does not go away but, apart from treatment, only gets worse.

Maybe it was my naive attitude or perhaps it was because I was feeling better—my eyesight had returned and my sense of touch was back intact—but I refused to accept the doctor's dire prognosis. Instead, I filled my mind with thoughts about improving my next album while continuing to tour. Although the doctor had warned that I might experience unusual fatigue, he had not cautioned me against singing.

Still, I worried privately that I wouldn't be able to sing as I normally could because of the MS. As yet, I had no idea how MS might affect my voice, so I decided to take precautions. I enrolled in vocal lessons in Nashville with a great teacher, invested in keeping my voice healthy and exercised.

Luke and I were listening to some of the playbacks for songs recorded for my new album, when he stopped the music. Luke turned, looked at me, and asked, "Are you taking vocal lessons?"

I worried that Luke had heard about my doctor's appointments, since I had missed a couple of days recording with Byron. I fretted that my secret might be exposed.

"Yeah, why do you ask?"

"You need to quit those," Luke said. "Something doesn't sound like you. Something has changed."

"Luke, I'm one of your few artists who does not have to take time off from touring to rest my voice," I reminded him. "Vocal lessons help keep my voice strong." I knew that several other Mercury artists were having to come off the road because they were suffering vocal problems.

Luke acknowledged the truth of what I was saying, but his comment got inside my head. I doubted myself in a way I never had. Indeed, Luke's statement nagged at me throughout the recording process of my second album, *Men and Mascara*.

I knew that I had MS, but Luke didn't know it.

Although I had neglected my doctor's admonitions and had stuffed his information in my drawer, I wondered if the stress of recording a second album was exacerbating the effects of the disease. *Maybe Luke was right. Maybe my voice has changed.*

My new producer, Byron Gallimore, and I were learning to work well together. He was the consummate professional who seemed to know what he wanted before we even began. Once I grew more comfortable with his style, I found myself depending more and more on his opinion of what was right or wrong for me, even when it clashed with my own ideas. That was probably a mistake, but we recorded some great music together.

Still, there was something missing, something almost magical that I had experienced on my first album, and I longed for that same sort of feeling. I wanted to hear him say, "I believe it." He never did.

When the magic wasn't there, I sloughed it off as maturity. I was now a known recording artist, and I couldn't expect to be as starry-eyed and enthusiastic about my second album as I'd been about my first. This was, after all—and never forget it—the music business.

Except, for me, it wasn't. It was my *life*. I wanted to make a record that expressed ideas or life experiences that people could relate to—that *I* could relate to.

I breathed a sigh of relief when the album was finally completed. To celebrate, I decided to go get my hair done before going back on the road. I was sitting in the hair salon when Jason Owen came in to find me.

"Luke wants you to add a song to the record," he told me.

"My record is done," I said, somewhat surprised.

"Well, here's a song, 'Girl Next Door.'" Jason handed me a CD. "Luke would really like you to do it, so just listen to it." My hairstylist had a CD player, and he played the song for me while I was still in his chair. I held my head down and closed my eyes as I listened. The song had a pop sound, but I wasn't too worried about that. I knew we could transform it into something more country. But I couldn't connect with the lyrics. Moreover, the lyrics weren't something I would say in my music. They compared a girl who was the popular prom queen and cheerleader with one who was not, and the bitter resentment stewing between the two of them. At one point, the lyrics even suggested physical violence. I say a lot of bold things in my music, but I'd never say that I want to hit another woman—or a man, either, for that matter.

The song ended, and I opened my eyes and raised my head. I looked at Jason. "What do you think of it?" I asked him.

"I like it," he said. "I think you'll do a great job on it." I thanked him for his opinion, but I didn't share it.

Luke called me shortly after and said, "If you will do this for me, I promise, even if the song doesn't work, I'll make the record work." Apparently, Luke's boss, Doug Morris, higher in the Universal echelon, loved the song and wanted a female artist to record it. Luke decided that artist should be me.

But "Girl Next Door" was not even a country song. It was a pop song, previously recorded by a pop group. About that time, however, a number of country artists were enjoying great success by appealing to a pop music audience as well as country music fans. With so much riding on my new album, the big shots at the record company decided that tweaking my image in that direction might send me soaring to astronomical heights.

I understood that, but I remained unconvinced. Not to mention that there were the practical issues of getting the song recorded. "I'm leaving tomorrow morning for California. My flight is already booked."

"Don't worry about it," Jason said. "I've changed your flight."

"I don't even know the song. I need time to learn it."

"Okay," Jason said. "Take it home and learn it."

"Is Byron available on such short notice?" I asked, grasping at straws.

"No, but James Stroud is available. Meet him at the studio tomorrow morning. James is going to produce the song."

It was becoming obvious to me that I really had no choice. It seemed as though the record label had already decided that I was going to add the song to my album, whether I wanted to or not. They had even gone into the studio and recorded the music tracks for the song.

The following morning, I met James Stroud in the recording studio. Although I had been introduced to him previously at the party celebrating my gold album, I didn't really know James. He had a reputation as a stellar producer and had recently scored great successes with Toby Keith, but James and I had never before worked together. Meeting him one-on-one, I liked him immediately. James was all business, but he possessed a down-home, Southern charm that set me at ease. Still, I wasn't happy that our initial creative efforts together would be on a song I'd first heard less than eighteen hours earlier.

"I'm sorry, I don't even know this song," I admitted to him. "And I don't love it. It's a pop song, not country."

Those were not the words a hit producer wants to hear, but James was gracious and confident. "Don't worry. I recorded some banjo and Dobro at the front of it. I think it will work. Trust me."

I sang through the song a few times, and it was clear that I didn't know it well enough to pour myself into it.

I left the studio still not liking the song, but James seemed pleased. "It will be fine," he said. "You did some great vocal tracks. I can work with them and put it together."

Ron Shapiro called me later that day. "They love it," he said. "Do you like it?"

"No, not really, Ron," I said with a sigh. I paced back and forth in my hotel room as we talked. "To me, it doesn't sound believable."

The label put out "Men and Mascara," the title song, as the first single. It was well received by radio program directors and deejays as well as Country Music Television. Mercury followed with "Girl Next Door"—and the deejays and programmers gave it a thumbs-down. They saw it as a departure from my previous album and not really who I was. And they were right.

Ironically, not long after that, Taylor Swift put out a similar song, comparing a glamour girl and a plain Jane, and it was a huge hit. It worked well for her. But not for me.

Making matters worse, Mercury decided that they wanted to use a more pop-music approach to the cover art. The label wanted to use a photo of my legs rather than my face. The photographer had taken a series of shots of me in a pastel mint-green dress, with lace around the bottom. The dress came down below my knees in a soft, sophisticated look. I wore a beautiful pair of stylish high-heeled shoes with the dress. I wasn't opposed to the look, but to put my calves and feet on the front cover without the rest of my body, and especially my face, made no sense to me.

In those days, I did everything that the record company asked me to do. But I was beginning to realize that these people were trying to make me into somebody who was not the real me. So I balked. I refused to approve the cover. "People don't know me well enough for us to do something like that," I argued.

The record company execs disagreed—and they ran with the cover without my approval.

When Mama saw it, she was furious. "Why didn't they put your face on the cover?" she asked.

"I don't know, Mama," I replied despondently. "I guess they thought my legs would sell more albums."

13

Goodbye, Girl Next Door

Throughout the spring and summer of 2005, the record company and I did everything possible to promote "Girl Next Door" before the release of the full album in 2006. Having worked in Luke's office, I knew the intense dance done by record companies and radio stations. Certain radio stations wielded enormous power when it came to the success or failure of an album or single, and within the stations, certain deejays and program directors reigned supreme.

When I worked for Mercury, at the beginning of each week, I delivered the program sheets to Luke, Jason, and the other members of the promotional team. Luke pored carefully over those radio sheets.

"Why isn't that station adding Shania?" I'd hear him

ask. "Where's Reba's single on this list?" he wanted to know. "Why aren't they playing it?"

So as we were promoting "Girl Next Door," I asked to receive copies of those radio sheets. I wanted to know what stations were playing and if a station for whom I had played a free show had added my single to its playlist—or not.

In Kansas City, one radio station had always been good to me, so I was playing a huge outdoor country music festival sponsored by the station. The program director was Mike Kennedy, and Mike always played my music.

It was the first time that I would perform "Girl Next Door" for the Kansas City radio audience. The people at Mercury emphatically told me, "You have to do this right. It is important that the station adds the single." They reiterated, "No pressure, of course. But this station could make or break your record."

"If you can just get a number-one radio hit on the Billboard chart," Luke promised, "then your life will change. You just need one."

As is often the case at those huge music festivals, in Kansas City, my band members did a sound check and then had to leave their instruments onstage or backstage, waiting for our set. It was a sweltering hot day, with the sun beating on the instruments, causing the strings to go out of tune.

By the time we came to "Girl Next Door," my lead guitar player was so out of tune, I couldn't even find the right notes to hit. It was a total train wreck. I was embarrassed, and for a moment, I wondered if I was getting punked, if somebody from another band were pulling a joke on us.

Finally, I stopped the performance in the middle of the

first verse of the song. "You know what?" I said to the audience. "We're not in tune. I don't know why we're having this problem, but I don't want the first time you hear this song to be wrong. We're gonna stop and tune up, and then play it right."

We moved on to the next song and then came back to "Girl Next Door" later in the show. We needed a great performance for the station to add the song, and we simply didn't pull it off. I felt horrible.

I fretted to Haley, my Mercury radio representative. "Please explain to the radio guys what happened out there. The heat was the problem, not the song."

"I'll tell them," Haley promised.

But the Kansas City station did not add "Girl Next Door." I felt as though our performance at the festival there had been the kiss of death on the song. For the first time since before I'd gotten the record deal, fear that my career was taking a downward turn took hold in my heart.

The breakdown in my confidence showed up in the worst way. I was on the road promoting *Men and Mascara* when two musicians and I visited a major Philadelphia radio station. Bill Catino, a senior radio PR guy with Universal Music Group, accompanied me to the interview and stressed to me the importance of this station playing my single, "Girl Next Door."

The interview went well. Then the deejay wanted us to sing on-air live, so my two guitar players and I positioned ourselves in front of the microphones. My heart began racing wildly, practically in panic-attack mode. I could hardly breathe, and I felt as though I couldn't get enough air to sing.

"Please sing really loud," I whispered to the musicians. "I don't think I can sing this song this morning." They nodded knowingly.

I'm sure I sang terribly, but the guys covered for me. Despite their efforts, I knew the radio station would not add the single.

I made a hasty exit from the studio, trying to get my heart to calm down, fretting that Luke's comment was coming true—and maybe the MS was affecting my voice.

It would be a long time before I could overcome the damage done by Luke's one innocuous comment about how my voice had changed. He may have meant it merely as constructive criticism, but it had hit me at a vulnerable time that left me less confident in my vocal performance. To avoid further panic attacks, for a while, I had to take anxiety medications even to be able to step onstage or to do a radio interview that required me to sing on-air.

Although I was disappointed at the poor response "Girl Next Door" received, still, good things were happening in my career during that time. My manager, Ron Shapiro, worked out a deal with the Wilhelmina Models talent agency to secure endorsement opportunities and commercial print advertisements in which I could appear. For one of my first print-ad photo sessions, Wilhelmina connected me to Red Baron Pizza, who also paid me for some concerts. I also appeared in ads for Fuze health drinks, LensCrafters eyewear, and even did a television commercial for Jimmy Dean's healthy breakfast foods.

For most commercials, all I had to do was show up on time. The photographers and advertisers supplied a makeup artist, the clothing and shoes I was to wear, even a hairstylist. The work was relatively easy since, in most cases, I was basically getting all dressed up to do a photo shoot, something I loved to do anyway. And they *paid* me for that!

The beauty about doing commercials was that the income did not apply toward my deficit account with Mercury. My manager received a percentage of the client's fee paid to me, and of course, Wilhelmina received a hefty amount for its services, but after them, God, and the IRS, any money I made from modeling was mine! Having worked for free for several years, it was a tremendous blessing to actually earn some money that I could keep. More importantly, thanks to my work with Wilhelmina, I finally had some money in my savings account. I was able to buy Mama some nice things, give bonuses to my band members and crew, and become involved with a number of charitable activities.

I also participated in a nationwide campaign for Clinique, in which I was paired with Barbados-born R&B artist Rihanna to promote the fragrance Happy. I recorded the song "Happy" in New York and appeared in Clinique events at stores all over America, taking photos with customers and signing bottles of perfume.

Ron cautiously and carefully watched out for me, making sure that I did not become involved in any commercials that would be counterproductive for me. The only time he and I clashed over a commercial opportunity was a food ad for Zaxby's that I wanted to do, but Ron felt it was tacky. I love Zaxby's food, but the script and storyboard for the commercial called for a pretty girl to eat a sandwich and have some of the juices drip down her chin.

"You cannot be seen like that," Ron said, shaking his head. He did not feel the ad was appropriate for me, so we turned it down, despite a potentially lucrative paycheck.

Ironically, around that same time, the fast-food restaurants Carl's Jr. and Hardee's incorporated similar, but much more provocative, ideas in their television commercials featuring Paris Hilton, Heidi Klum, and later, Charlotte McKinney's infamous Super Bowl commercials. Critics said the restaurant chains were selling sex rather than burgers, and feminists cried foul. Although the Zaxby's ads were nowhere near as controversial, I was thankful that Ron kept me far away from a potential scandal.

In the late spring of 2005, Jason Owen learned that the ABC-TV morning show *Good Morning America* wanted to do a new theme song, "Good to Go." I had been a guest on the show previously promoting "Break Down Here" and my first album. The producers and the cast—Diane Sawyer, Robin Roberts, Charlie Gibson, and Tony Perkins—loved the dreams-come-true-story of the receptionist becoming the music recording star. So Jason recommended me for the song—an upbeat, energizing theme—and ABC agreed.

"Are you comfortable with James Stroud producing the song?" Jason asked.

James and I had worked well together on "Girl Next Door," and it wasn't his fault that the single failed. I was glad James would be the producer. James recorded the tracks for "Good to Go" in Nashville, but ABC requested us to record the vocals in New York City.

Once again, I received the song the night before, but it was a fun song to sing. I learned it overnight, and ABC flew me to New York to record it the following day. Monica, the show's talent producer, remained with us in the recording studio, along with several ABC executives. That made me slightly nervous, but in his easygoing, Southern way, James did a fantastic job of setting me at ease. We recorded the vocals, and the song came out great. We debuted the song on air on May 7, 2005, just ten days before the Academy of Country Music Awards show in Las Vegas. *Good Morning America* used the song as the show's theme song for two full seasons.

We later even did a video in which Diane, Robin, Charlie, Tony, and I were dancing all around the studio as I sang the song. I loved Diane. She was so classy and a real people person, as was Robin Roberts. Tony Perkins, the weather guy, was fun, too, but Charlie Gibson intimidated me because he was so serious. He apparently saw himself as "the news guy" and didn't seem too thrilled to be dancing around the studio in a music video. But he did it, and we all had fun.

A few weeks later, I traveled to Las Vegas for the 2005 Academy of Country Music Awards, held at the Mandalay Bay Resort on the Las Vegas Strip. The show was broadcast live by CBS. I sat next to Miranda Lambert, and we traded guesses about which female artists would take home the most prestigious awards that night. Miranda was a relatively new artist at the time, having finished third behind Buddy Jewell and Arthur Martinez in the 2003 *Nashville Star* competition. She had recently signed with Sony/Epic Records, and I felt sure it was only a matter of time before she soared to the top.

She was especially kind to me, rooting for me to win the Top New Artist Award, for which I was nominated along with almost the same group as the CMA's Horizon Award in late 2004—Big & Rich, Josh Turner, Gretchen Wilson—as well as Josh Gracin. I appreciated Miranda's support, but I think we both knew that Gretchen was going to steal the show, which she did, winning both the Top New Artist Award and the Top Female Vocalist Award, beating out singers Martina McBride, Sara Evans, Lee Ann Womack, and Terri Clark. Kenny Chesney won the Entertainer of the Year Award.

Despite my recent anxiety and loss of self-confidence, I enjoyed celebrating the success of my peers. Something about getting my eyes off myself made me feel better. Instead of getting down on myself, I was determined to work harder so I could be sitting in the award show seats again the following year.

The 2005 Country Music Association Awards show was

held in New York City. Jason Owen, my trusted PR person, picked out both the song I'd perform and my clothes.

I had done "Break Down Here" on the first CMA Awards show at which I performed, so the label didn't want me to do that song again. I suggested a song I'd written called "Smile," which started out with my voice only, followed by a very country-sounding guitar lick. Instead, the label preferred that I do the up-tempo song that I wrote, "First to Never Know."

My discomfort went from bad to worse when I put on the tight-fitting dress Jason had chosen for me.

"I can hardly breathe," I fretted.

"You look great," Jason said. He ran his eyes up and down my body, as though inspecting an inmate being processed into prison. "Just be sure to hold in your stomach while you sing," Jason cautioned me.

I rolled my eyes and said, "Thanks, Jason." I never felt that I was thin enough, and holding in my stomach was just another thing I had to think about. I was already worried about my performance. I was doing a song that I didn't ordinarily do, with a fiddle player who was not part of our band, and wearing shoes that didn't fit. I was a nervous wreck.

Despite my anxiety, I felt the CMA show went great. And I held in my tummy as I sang so my 108-pound body would look slimmer on television.

Luke told me at a party after the CMA Awards that radio stations did not really like the new song, "First to Never Know." That was disappointing, since Luke was the one who had wanted me to sing that song on the awards show!

A few months later, after "Girl Next Door" continued to fizzle, Ron called me and said, "Luke says he is not going to push anything else on your record."

"What?" I was surprised. "That's not what he told me. He promised that he would support the album whether the song worked or not."

"Maybe so," Ron said. "But apparently he's changed his mind."

I was devastated. I had done exactly what Luke had asked me to do, and I was extremely disappointed that he was no longer fighting for our record—and my career.

It hurt to have a song rejected by radio, but it hurt even more when Luke did not live up to his promise to me.

14

Men and Mascara— They Always Run!

Maintaining a social life while making and promoting music is an interesting balancing act. I was young and single, and the record company was hyping me as the accessible girl next door. They never discouraged any media coverage—true or false—about whom I might be dating.

For instance, at the 2005 CMA Awards, Kenny Chesney and I had briefly encountered each other backstage in my dressing room before the show. He popped his head inside the door, and said, "Hey, I'm Kenny. Loved your song. Good luck tonight." Kenny was nominated for two awards, Top Male Vocalist and Entertainer of the Year. We exchanged congratulations for each other's nominations, hugged, and went on our way.

But the cameras were everywhere, and the next thing I knew, rumors were flying all over Nashville and in the tabloids that Kenny and I were dating and were soon to be engaged!

A few weeks later, when we were both back in Nashville, Kenny sent me a text message. "Hey, do you want to come over? We're dating!"

I laughed and sent him a message back. "I'm working in the studio right now."

"Well, just come on by when you're done."

"Okay, I'll do that. I'll be coming from Music Row. Do you want me to bring any food or anything?"

"Yeah, can you bring me a White Castle hamburger?"

"Really?" I knew that Kenny maintained a strict diet and exercise regimen.

"Nah," he said. "I'm just kidding ya."

Kenny's house was incredibly beautiful and immaculately maintained. "Do you live in this big house by yourself?" I asked him, as he showed me around.

"Uh-huh." Kenny smiled. "That's your closet right there. That's where your clothes would be," he joked as he showed me through the gorgeous master bedroom.

"Oh really?" I said, smiling in return.

Kenny showed me his many music awards, and I was truly impressed. I didn't stay long. I think we both knew that my visit was merely a whimsical dream for our publicists. Everywhere I went people asked me, "Are you dating Kenny Chesney?"

"No, I'm not," I said.

"Yes, you are!" my friends in South Carolina said. "We saw it in a magazine."

Maybe so, but contrary to reports in the media, Kenny and I never dated, and we certainly weren't engaged. But we are still friends, and I admire his talent and great sense of humor.

Though I encountered many interesting guys, I was still devoted to Jack, the NFL football player I'd met in 2004. Yet he did not reciprocate emotionally with me. In fact, he often gave the impression that he didn't want to be seen with me in public, and he never introduced me as his girlfriend. He never offered to pay for me to visit him; I always paid my own way. And he didn't invite me to his Fourth of July lake party—even though, I later found out, the guest list included a number of swimsuit-clad girls. That should have been enough to drive me away from Jack, but I hung on to hope that he would take more of an interest in our relationship.

Although he earned a fabulous salary, we didn't go out to fancy places or eat at the nicest restaurants. Instead we ate at small pizza shops or picked up food from a local grocery store. The only place we ever went together where Jack might be known was his gym.

I understood the demands on Jack because of his career. He was extremely disciplined about his physical conditioning and practice schedule. I could relate to both of those, since I was on the road a lot, as well, so I made a greater effort to go see him at his convenience and on my own dime.

On one occasion I had a few days free on my schedule, so I called Jack and suggested that I visit with him and his family. He said, "No, you can't come. I have to work out this week." That was odd to me, because on previous trips, Jack and I had worked out together.

On another occasion, I was walking with Jack to his car when he pressed the wrong button on his keyless remote. Rather than the doors unlocking, his trunk popped open. In his trunk, he had a beautifully wrapped present—for one of his former girlfriends!

I was furious. I could feel myself seething with anger, more than I'd ever felt before. The "crazy girl" came out of me. "Why do you have a gift for her?" I asked. "I'm going to call her right now. Give me her number."

"She's just a friend," Jack said.

I called her and said, "I just want you to know that Jack and I are dating."

She denied that she was seeing him, but my suspicions remained. I felt sure that Jack had betrayed my trust.

I had to face the truth: Jack was wrong for me. Finally, I worked up the courage to say, "No more. I'm done." But he had wounded me deeply, in ways that I wondered would ever heal. Looking back, I realize that I allowed him to do it. I put up with his nonsense and did not demand better of him. I had neglected a basic lesson in relationships: it's your responsibility to teach someone how to treat you, so keep your expectations high.

You might think that I had learned my lesson, that when I

saw red flags around a relationship, I would run in the opposite direction. You might think that, but you'd be wrong.

~

Not long after I broke up with Jack, I played an outdoor show
in Tennessee. Afterward, my road manager, Jeff Gossett,
said, "I have a friend who wants to meet you. He has a gift
he wants to give to you."

"Okay, fine," I said. Even though he was a stranger, if the
guest was a friend of Jeff's, I didn't mind meeting him.

Jeff introduced me to his friend Cooper, who came on
my bus to greet me. Cooper was tall, good-looking, and
dressed in nice jeans, a country-style shirt, and cowboy
boots. He was a great conversationalist, and I enjoyed talking with him.

"Could I take you to dinner sometime?" Cooper asked
before he left.

"Well, maybe, when I'm home," I said. "That might
be fun."

Cooper knew how to get in touch with me through Jeff,
so when I was home in Nashville, he called and asked me out
to dinner at a lovely, upscale restaurant. This was already
looking better than Jack.

Unlike Jack, Cooper actually wined and dined me, and
he treated my family well, too, taking them out to dinner
and bringing them gifts.

But then I noticed his drinking. He somehow managed
to down twelve strong alcoholic beverages during a cross-
country flight. Twelve! I counted them. That was bad enough,

but he could still function despite being obviously impaired. His drinking reminded me of Daddy, and it scared me.

One night he drank so much I had to take him home. As I got him settled into his condo, I noticed he was receiving numerous text messages on his cell phone. The messages were all from the same person—another female country artist.

I confronted him, and he did not deny that he had been with her. I broke off my relationship with Cooper.

Unlike Jack, Cooper had given me some expensive jewelry as presents. When we broke up, I gave it all back to him. Cooper came to my home, in an effort to win me back. We sat on the couch in the living room, and I sat stoically with one of my dogs, Lucie, in my lap. Cooper apologized and promised me the moon. "I'll do anything, baby," he said. "I'll never be unfaithful again. It didn't mean anything. You're the woman for me, the only one I want."

I didn't say much, but as Cooper went on and on, apparently Lucie had heard enough. She snapped at Cooper and bit him right on the nose! I couldn't believe my eyes. Lucie was one of the sweetest, most docile dogs I'd ever been around, and for her to snap at Cooper was totally out of character. Yet it was so perfectly right!

Cooper left shortly after Lucie bit him, and I was glad. I couldn't help thinking of the line in the title song from my own album: "Men and mascara always run."

15

Carolina Bred: California Bound

In 2005, I met the highly regarded television movie producer Ellyn Williams. Ellyn was familiar with my music, and when she learned more about my story, moving from receptionist to a successful recording artist, she was convinced it would make a great movie for Sony Pictures and the Lifetime television network. At the time, I was signed to Creative Artists Agency, and Ellyn was, too, so it seemed like a perfect fit.

She came to Nashville, and we discussed the possibility of working together. Of course, I did not tell Ellyn "the rest of the story"—that I now knew I had a debilitating disease.

That wasn't unusual. I was still firmly in denial. I said nothing about the MS to anyone. The only people who knew

I had the disease were my doctor, Mama, my sister Lorie, and me. And Mama and I never talked about it.

Ellyn secured the services of Keith Glover, a scriptwriter, to work together with me on the story for a movie about my life, with the working title *Girl Next Door*. My record company was fully on board, still hopeful that the movie could help turn the song by that same title into a hit for me—and for them.

Part of the writer's responsibilities was to interview my extended family members to get a bit of my family background. The first writer with whom Ellyn teamed me happened to be African American.

Keith Glover traveled to South Carolina to meet my grandparents, who were steeped in old-style racism. Of course, they wouldn't call it that. As far as they were concerned, they simply shared the attitudes of most of their neighbors. They had probably never had an African American inside their home in their entire lifetime. Mama tried to delicately prepare Pawpaw for the Lifetime writer's visit.

"The writer wants to interview you," Mama said.

"That's fine. I can do that."

"Well, he's going to have to ask you a lot of questions."

"Dat's all right," Pawpaw said. "I got that."

"Well, there's one other thing," Mama ventured.

"What's dat? Spit it out, what is it?"

"The writer is a black man," Mama told him.

"That's okay. I'll be nice to him. If it's important to Julie, I can handle it."

When the writer arrived at Pawpaw's house, my grandfather did his best to be hospitable. "Come on out back with me to my garden," he invited the writer. "I want to show ya my t'maters."

Keith interviewed Mawmaw and Pawpaw, and they got along fine. In what Pawpaw considered as the ultimate gesture of friendship, he said to Keith, "I know yer black, and I ain't got a thing against ya. Yer welcome in my house anytime."

That was the culture in which I grew up. Racism—subtle or overt—was not only tolerated; it was expected. The writer understood those endemic prejudices, and he handled the situation with tremendous grace and aplomb. Not only did he do a good job on the initial interviews, but he and Mama remain friends to this day.

I continued touring full time throughout 2006, 2007, and 2008. When the full album, *Men and Mascara*, released in 2006, I got back on the tour bus and hit the road hard for the next three years in support of both of my Mercury albums. Still, no one in my professional life knew I had MS. Other than fatigue and occasional numbness in my hands, I didn't have any obvious residual physical problems. Most of the time I felt great, so it was easy to continue touring. Not only did I tour much of the United States, but I also did two concert tours in Europe and a number of country music festivals in Canada.

I rarely even thought of the MS. It did not affect my singing voice in any way that I noticed. (The temporary voice strain I experienced while recording my second album was a result of anxiety, not MS.) Nor did I have any further incidents such as the one I'd experienced in the club the night I lost my vision and couldn't hold on to the microphone. I could still drive a car without problems. I didn't take any medications, and the doctor did not follow up with me. I sure wasn't about to follow up with him.

Maybe my neurologist knew that I was in denial and that I had to come to terms with the disease and accept it. Or maybe he wanted me to make the decision to follow through with a treatment regimen in my own time. Regardless, I did nothing to counteract the lesions that, like the alien bacteria in a bad B movie, continued attacking my brain. Mostly, I avoided thinking about it. I continued my strict diet and exercise routine.

I was thin—maybe too thin—thanks to my record company's insistence that I maintain a ridiculously toned figure. I noticed one day when I was working out with my trainer that I couldn't hold the hand weights for long. That was alarming to me, but I chose to ignore it.

The symptoms persisted, and occasionally, while working out, I had to apologize to my trainer because I couldn't lift the weights that I normally handled with ease. I offered excuses about being tired. I knew something was wrong, but I refused to acknowledge it, still hoping it would go away.

Despite our earlier excitement, due to some creative changes and Hollywood wheeling and dealing, the movie project didn't really get off the ground until 2009. The film company brought in Tom Rickman, who had written the script for the Loretta Lynn story *Coal Miner's Daughter.* Tom worked out of Los Angeles, and Ellyn suggested that it would be helpful for me to carve out six weeks or so from my schedule to work directly with Tom on the script.

"You could do it long distance from Nashville, but it would be better if you could come to Los Angeles during that time," she suggested.

"Six weeks?" I asked. "I think I could do that. I know I have some concert dates out west. The guys at Creative Artists Agency can probably help make that happen."

"Yes, I think that should be fine," Ellyn said. "Unless you want to stay longer and take some acting lessons." She smiled at me. "I'm planning to have you star in your own movie."

16

Great Bruton

A few weeks before I was scheduled to leave for Los Angeles to work on the movie, I was invited to sing "The Star-Spangled Banner" prior to the NASCAR race at the Atlanta Motor Speedway. Although I had lived in South Carolina, where auto racing is tremendously popular, I had never been to a NASCAR race. Nor had I ever sung the national anthem to such an enormous crowd—more than one hundred thousand people at the raceway, and millions more on television.

Afterward, a sharply dressed racetrack staff member wearing a sports jacket and tie approached me. "The owner of the track would like to meet you and your mom and thank you for singing the anthem."

We followed the steward to a lavish corporate suite high above the racetrack. Mama and I went inside the suite and were introduced to Bruton Smith, a rather rotund man in his eighties, wearing large-rimmed, gold-tinted glasses. Actually, it seemed that everything around Bruton was gold—the furniture, the dishes, the glasses, the cutlery . . . everything.

"I just want to thank you for singing the anthem today," Bruton said.

"Well, thank you for inviting me," I said. I looked around at the huge catering area in the suite. "This is amazing!"

We talked for a while, and he asked me about my future plans. I told him that I'd soon be going to Los Angeles to work on a movie script. He seemed quite interested and told me that he had a number of rental properties, including one in LA where Mick Jagger had once lived.

"I have a lot of friends in Nashville too," Bruton said. "I own some car dealerships there. In fact, you've probably bought a car from me and didn't know it."

"No, I'm sure I didn't," I responded. "I have a Honda. What sort of dealerships do you have?"

"Cadillac, Mercedes. . . ."

"Well, I'm in the market for a new car," I joked.

Bruton handed me a business card. "Here's my friend at the Mercedes dealership," he said. "Tell him I sent you, and he will give you exceptional service."

When I returned to Nashville, I stopped by the dealership Bruton had told me about. The manager did indeed give me a good deal, and I bought a new black Mercedes C300 for not much more than I was paying for my Honda. It wasn't gold, but I felt sure Bruton would have approved.

As my scriptwriting adventure in LA drew nearer, I called Ron Shapiro, my manager in New York. "Where am I supposed to live?" I asked.

"Mercury won't cover that bill," Ron said with a laugh. "And it would be too expensive to stay in hotels. You could rent someplace on a weekly basis, but that would be pricey too. Why don't you contact Bruton Smith and see if you can stay in the house he has for sale there?" I remembered telling Ron about Bruton's rental property.

"I don't want to bother him," I said.

"Julie, you are going to be there for six weeks," Ron reminded me. "Housing in Los Angeles is much more expensive than Nashville."

I agreed, so I called Bruton and said, "I'm moving to LA for a while, and I was wondering if I could rent your house."

"Honey," he drawled, "you can stay in my place." I felt as though I could almost see his eyes gleaming. "It's for sale, but nobody is living in it right now."

"How much is the rent?" I asked.

"Honey," he said again, "you don't need to pay me anything."

I should have known that wasn't true. Oh, the things that naive, single females in country music want to believe!

In January 2009, I moved to Bruton's empty home in Los Angeles. It was enormous, with more rooms than I had ever

seen in one home. It was fully furnished and boasted exquisite landscaping and a gorgeous pool area. I had never visited
such a palatial house, much less lived in such a place.

I was a little nervous, too, since I had never lived alone.
I'd always had my sisters, college roommates, or Mama living
with me, so I invited various friends to come visit me every
weekend. I even had someone bring Lucie, one of my dogs,
out to LA. I didn't want to be alone in Bruton's big house.
Perhaps as a reflection of the country girl still in me, despite
the enormity and opulence of the house, I mostly stayed in
only two rooms: the bedroom and the kitchen.

I had lived in Bruton's home for nearly six weeks when my
friend Renee came to visit and help me celebrate my birthday. We were getting ready to go out for a special birthday
dinner when Bruton called.

"Honey," Bruton said, "what are you doing?"

"My friend Renee and I are going to go out for dinner," I
said. "It's my birthday."

"Oh, that's wonderful! There's a great restaurant in the
Beverly Hills Hotel," he said. "I'm here in town, and I want
to celebrate with you, so I'll take you ladies there for dinner."

I really wasn't excited about including octogenarian
Bruton in our plans, but we were staying in his home. It was
difficult to exclude him without being terribly rude, and I
didn't want to do that. "Okay, fine," I finally acquiesced.

We went to the restaurant at the Beverly Hills Hotel,
but I noticed that Bruton didn't have any luggage, and he

didn't check into the hotel. "Aren't you staying at the hotel?" I asked.

"No, honey," Bruton drawled. "I'm staying at my house tonight."

Again, it was his home, and he certainly had a right to stay there. I wondered, however, whether Renee and I should leave while he was in town. That seemed silly since the cavernous home had more than enough space for all of us. Still, I felt a little uncomfortable about that arrangement; something didn't sit well with me.

At dinner, Renee and I sent text messages back and forth. "What are we going to do?" I texted frantically.

When we got back to the house, Bruton went inside with us. I was hoping he'd be tired and ready to fall asleep, so I said, "I'm going to take Lucie on a walk."

"I'll come with you," Renee said. We took Lucie on a really long walk. When we returned to the house, Bruton was still awake.

"Come on up here," he called from his bedroom. "I have a present for your birthday."

I hesitated, then I slowly walked up the grand staircase, not knowing what sort of gift I might find waiting for me. Once upstairs, I discovered that Bruton did, indeed, have a birthday card and a $500 Macy's department store gift card for me. Relieved, I thanked Bruton for his generosity and kindness and headed back downstairs.

"When are you coming to bed, honey?" Bruton called after me.

"Ah, I'll be right back," I said, and hurried down to the guest bedroom where Renee and I were staying.

"Renee, we need to lock ourselves in this bedroom with Lucie and stay in this room all night!" I said.

We didn't come out all night long. We got up early the next morning, before Bruton woke up, and we went on a long hike. He called me later that day.

"I sold the house," Bruton said. "You need to come home and pack your stuff."

I had to get an apartment in Los Angeles before the end of the weekend, which was no easy task. The television network had paid me a small advance to secure my story, but I was still trying to be frugal since I was spending my own money. Frugal and LA are contradictory ideas, I soon discovered.

My friend Renee helped me find a fabulous apartment near The Grove, a popular section of town, but I had to sign a six-month lease to get it. I also had to rent furniture. I felt stressed because I was doling out so much money, but I didn't really mind because I felt that at last, I was investing in myself. It was the first time I'd ever lived completely on my own, and I enjoyed my freedom. The apartment complex was gated, so I felt safe. I used the gift card Bruton had given me to buy sheets, towels, and basic things for my apartment.

I went to work with Tom Rickman, meeting regularly with him regarding stories for the script. Meanwhile, Creative Artists Agency set me up at an acting school where I attended when I wasn't working with Tom. I was happy and loved the classes. I didn't really see myself becoming a movie star. I simply wanted to learn how to be a better actor because I wanted to do well on the film project.

My representative from Creative Artists Agency communicated with the acting school and received a report that I was doing very well with my classes. The CAA rep told Ron Shapiro, "Julie's doing so well that I think it would be good for her to do the next phase and continue the acting classes for another six months."

When Ron gave me that assessment, it was bittersweet. "Ron, I'm glad they think I can act, but it's really expensive to stay here," I said. "This is costing me a lot."

I had not planned on staying in California more than six weeks, then six months; now I was looking at being gone for more than a year.

Progress was slow, and we went through several revisions and iterations of the script. I was hemorrhaging money like water pouring out of a fire hydrant, spending my life savings to remain in California to work on the movie. Even though I wasn't getting paid, I felt sure the money would come back to me, because eventually, I would be paid by Sony for the Lifetime movie.

And then the bottom dropped out.

Near the end of 2009, the executives at Lifetime changed, and the company underwent a major restructuring. Many of the people with whom I had been working were gone. Shortly thereafter, I heard that Sony had put our movie on hold. That was extremely disconcerting to me, since I had already invested more than a year of my life and thousands of my own dollars to work on the project. Beyond that, I had taken a year off from touring, performing concerts, and writing music. I had to know whether this movie was going to happen.

I contacted Ellyn Williams, the executive producer on the movie, and expressed my concern. "Ellyn, what in the world is going on?" Ellyn seemed discouraged as she confirmed to me that Lifetime had placed our movie on hold.

"I know what it means to have a song on hold in Nashville," I said, "and it is usually a good thing. Maybe an artist wants to record your song. What does 'on hold' mean in the movie industry?" I held my breath as I waited for her response.

"It means that it might be as long as ten years before your movie gets made," Ellyn replied despondently.

Ellyn's response saddened me deeply, but I appreciated her honesty. All our signed contracts meant nothing. There was no legal recourse if the studio decided to ditch the project.

"What do you think I should do?" I asked.

"If it were me," she said, "I'd go back to Nashville. Work on your music, and we'll try to get this deal back together when the timing is right."

I thought about Ellyn's advice and realized that she was right. As much as I loved living in LA, it was expensive, and it was a pause in my music career. I needed to get back to the music in me. I wanted to write, record, and perform the songs inside me. As much as I enjoyed my acting classes and my independence in LA, I decided to pack up and move back to Nashville.

I returned home from California by Christmas 2009, and I immediately got busy writing new music. One of the people I was most excited to see—after Mama and Lorie, back home in Nashville—was Luke Lewis, head of Mercury Records, my music label. Ron Shapiro had kept him updated on my progress while I was in California. Luke had been supportive of the movie, and he had assured me that it could be a great opportunity to jump-start my music career again. Because Luke had always been in my corner prior to the "Girl Next Door" fiasco, I felt comfortable and confident that he would be equally excited to reconnect.

In late April, I called Luke and set up a meeting with him at his office. "I'm back!" I said, "and I'm ready to make a new record." I was excited to see him, so I took some new songs along with me, thinking that he might want to hear my new ideas.

Luke greeted me warmly, yet he was somewhat more reserved than usual. After some perfunctory conversation, catching up a bit, I wanted to play him some new songs I hoped to record.

"Before you play me any music, how is the movie going?" Luke asked.

"Well . . . it's on hold," I said.

"Okay, then I don't want to hear any of your new music," Luke said matter-of-factly. "Your recording career here is on hold too."

I was shocked. *What?*

Luke read the expression on my face. "Julie, we need the

movie to promote your music. Radio is not playing female artists as much right now, and we need the movie to break through that."

The look on Luke's face surprised me. He was not smiling or expressing hope or compassion—"Gee, Julie, I'm so sorry to hear that the movie is on hold," or something like that. Instead, he looked stern.

His words echoed through my mind: if the movie is on hold, *your recording career here is on hold too.* He was all business, and I understood that look, having been Luke's assistant.

"What does that mean for me?" I asked. I had recorded only two of the albums originally agreed to in my Mercury recording contract. I still had an agreement to record five more albums for the label.

Luke paused and then said, "I will release you from your contract with Mercury, and you can go do something else."

I was heartbroken. Luke had been like a father figure to me. For him to dismiss me so summarily cut deeply into my heart. I had trusted him. He was the only man, other than Brent, to believe in my dream. And now he was telling me to walk. It was harder to hear those words from Luke than it was to hear the doctor informing me that I had MS.

And there was that, too: I knew that I had MS. Luke still did not.

17

The Flood

On May 1, 2010—barely a week after Luke let me go—
we awakened shortly before eight o'clock to the sound
of someone pounding on our front door. Mama answered
and found our neighbor standing in the pouring rain, soaking wet.

"You need to move your cars out of the driveway right
now," he urged. "Get them to higher ground. The river is rising
rapidly, and this whole neighborhood is going to be flooded!"

Mama took one look and realized that our neighbor
wasn't exaggerating. Water already flowed down our street.

I had sprained my ankle a few days earlier on a running
trail, so Mama said, "You stay here, and Lorie and I will go
out and move the cars."

Mama and Lorie climbed in my Mercedes and started to back out. They had barely moved the car ten feet up the street when the car suddenly flooded with water. The car doors locked automatically, trapping them inside.

Mama later told me that she had looked at Lorie and said, "You better pray! I guess we're about to die." It reminded me of what she had told Marie on that turbulent plane ride: "When it's your time to go. . . ."

"No, we are not!" Lorie had yelled back.

Lorie and Mama kept jiggling the locks, and finally the locks popped open. By then the water was several feet deep and swirling all around them. Mama and Lorie struggled to get the car doors open and stepped out into the stream of ice-cold, filthy, rapidly flowing water, fighting the current with all their strength, inching toward our front door.

I came outside just in time to see my newly paid-off Mercedes floating away in the rushing waters. "Mama!" I cried. "My car!" I pointed at the car floating down the street. "And there goes your Honda too!" But there was no time to worry about the cars. The water was already above my knees and rising rapidly. I stretched out my arms as far as I could to help Lorie and Mama, who trudged through the waist-high water to the front steps. We made it back inside the house and closed the door quickly.

We ran to find anything we could use to help seal the doors and windows, hoping to keep the water out of the house. But it was all to no avail. The waters continued to rise downstairs.

We knew we had to get upstairs. The water was already higher than the electrical outlets, so we worried about getting electrocuted.

"I want to save my sewing machine," Mama yelled.

"I'll get it," Lorie called. Lorie went to retrieve Mama's most cherished material possession, and then she and Mama moved it upstairs a little further out of the water—at least for now. I grabbed the dogs, my computer, and a few family photographs and, with Mama's help, limped up the stairs as fast as my legs would go. I looked out the upstairs window and was shocked to see that the water had risen almost above the streetlight poles.

It was horrifying to look on helplessly and watch the waters rising higher and higher, our rapid heartbeats punctuated by the crackling sounds of the electric transformers at the nearby substations blowing up. Our electricity went out immediately.

Mama grabbed some Cheese Nips and Diet Cokes from the cupboard, and I stashed my phone, my driver's license, and a credit card into the running shorts I was wearing.

We didn't dare try to go outside the house; swimming to safety was out of the question. The cold water was racing all around our house, with chunks of debris, trees, snakes, dead animals, and even cars floating by. Phone service was nonexistent since the nearby cell towers were fried as well. Inside the house, we felt terribly isolated, but we tried to stay calm.

Although we knew we were in trouble, we had no idea that thousands of other people all over Nashville, including areas of downtown, were experiencing similar problems. Weather experts would later conclude that we were in the middle of a "thousand-year flood," a flood such as no living person had ever before experienced in our city. It was certainly unlike anything I'd ever seen firsthand.

It was a few hours before we heard a volunteer rescue team outside our house, slowly making their way up the street in a small motorized boat. It looked as though they already had aboard several other people they had rescued. The rescuers called out to us, "How many do you have in there?"

"We have three women and four dogs," I said.

"We can take you three," the leader said, "but we can't take the dogs unless they are in carriers. Put your dogs in carrying cages, and we'll go help some other people. There are some sick and elderly folks down the street. We're gonna help them, then we'll come back to get you in a while. Bring any medicine if you can get it and anything you absolutely need."

"Okay," I called back to them. "Please hurry."

"We will," the man promised and waved goodbye.

For the next six hours, we waited . . . and waited . . . and waited in the dark. We had no radio, television, or phone service. It was dead calm, eerily quiet, the only sound being the water rushing through our living room or the popping or crackling of another transformer blowing up.

Occasionally, we heard voices of the rescue team outside. "We haven't forgotten you," they'd call to us. "We'll be back."

Meanwhile, we tried to move some keepsake items and pictures upstairs, but the water downstairs was too dangerous, so we didn't get much. I went up to the attic and found two dog carriers and put one dog in one carrier and two in the other. Our smallest dog, Dixie, was a tiny, blind Pomeranian, so Mama simply stuffed Dixie in her shirt.

Somewhere around three o'clock in the afternoon, the rescue boat returned. The rescuers pulled the boat right through our front door. I stashed my medications in a plastic bag and put it inside my bra, and Mama and Lorie did the same. We had no clothes other than those on our bodies. We left everything else behind.

The water had risen high inside the house, but Mama, Lorie, and I were able to ease down into the water and descend just a few steps of the staircase connecting our lower floor and the upstairs. The volunteers tossed us life jackets, and we hurriedly put them on. The boat came up as close as they could get it, and we climbed in.

In trying to hoist one of the dog carriers, my sprained ankle hit the side of the boat and I could feel it crack. Pain shot through my ankle, but I was so cold and focused on getting the animals into the boat, running on adrenaline, that I barely noticed I had broken my ankle. We huddled in the flat-bottomed rescue boat and floated out of our house. Down the street, the rescuers stopped to pick up an older couple, along with a couple of our neighbors.

A young man, whom I guessed to be around twenty-five years of age, climbed into the boat. He looked at our dogs and started to cry.

"What's wrong?" I asked him.

Through his tears, he said, "They made me leave my dog. He's a big dog, a Lab, so they wouldn't let me bring him."

My heart hurt for him. There were no words that could console him.

The volunteer rescue team took us to an evacuation center a few miles from our flooded home. Cots lined the shelter that was crowded with people clutching what little of their personal belongings they had been able to carry out of their homes. Somebody arrived at the center, bringing a supply of water.

"There's electrical power at the Kroger grocery store," the driver said. That piqued my imagination. I felt sure that if we could get there, my cell phone would work, and I could call some friends for help. My ankle was hurting like mad, and the swelling had increased. I knew I needed to get to a doctor soon.

"Can somebody give us a ride to Kroger?" I asked.

A fellow driving a 4x4 pickup truck offered us a ride. "I'll get you there," he said. "Hop in." Mama, Lorie, and I climbed into his truck, along with our dogs.

The store was only a few miles away, and just as I had hoped, when we arrived there, my cell phone service came back on. I called Anita, one of my good friends, and I also called Jason Collum, my bandleader. Jason had been playing drums with my band since 2006, and he and I had recently become close.

Both Jason and Anita offered to help, but I wasn't sure how our four dogs would get along with Anita's two Yorkies. Jason lived on a hill all the way on the other side of Nashville, but he generously suggested that we come there, and he and his brother would stay at his recording studio, which was located in an older home in Franklin. That seemed to be a better alternative, at least for the next few days, until we could get some clothes and figure things out.

Jason drove across town and picked us up within the hour. He took us to his home, and Mama, Lorie, and I collapsed on his couch, along with our four dogs.

The next day I went to a doctor, and he set my ankle and

gave me a safety boot to wear over it. We stayed at Jason's home for a few days, until we got the word from FEMA that it was safe to return to our home—though, of course, it was uninhabitable.

⁓

We had no idea what to expect as we approached our neighborhood. My heart sank as I saw the ruined and soiled furniture lining the streets leading to our home. Cars sat dislodged in random locations. It looked as though a bomb had exploded. *What are we going back to?* I wondered. *Will there be anything salvageable?* I felt as though our whole lives had been swept away.

The yard around our home was a mess. Trash from the river had washed up on what used to be our grass. Other people's belongings were strewn around the yard. The whole area possessed an eerie feeling.

The first thing I saw when we stepped up to our front door was a business card from Pastor Mike Shelton of Bellevue Baptist Church that read, "We were here while you were gone. We're thinking about you and praying for you. Please call us if you need anything."

Something about seeing that card spurred hope in my heart. Despite the fact that almost everything we owned was destroyed, and despite the nearly foot-high layer of mud in our home, I knew we were going to be okay.

Inside, the house was a wreck, the refrigerator had overturned in the water, our waterlogged furniture had been dislodged, the walls were stained with dirt and watermarks, and everything was a mess. Weirdly, other people's belongings had floated inside our house, as well, mixed with the mud and water. And, to top it off, back in March, Mama had received a notice that our flood insurance was no longer required—so she had canceled it in an attempt to save money.

I had no idea how, but we would start over. I felt I had been saved from the flood for a reason. Now I needed to be saved from myself.

Top left: Mama holding me at a couple months old. On our way to church in Lancaster, South Carolina.

Middle: Mama giving me a bath in MawMaw's sink at six and a half months old.

Bottom left: I am at MawMaw's house smiling on my way to church.

Bottom right: I am two years old in this picture with my sisters. We are getting ready to leave MawMaw's house for Easter service.

This is my first pageant photo in my first dress from the Diane Shop. I'm four years old.

I am in front of our Christmas tree with my sisters (Lorie, Marie, Julie).

Heading to a dance recital with my sisters!

My first performance on the Grand Ole Opry.

Right: I am singing at the Carolina Place Mall just outside of Charlotte, North Carolina, the day my first album was released.

Below: Little Jimmy Dickens introducing me on the Grand Ole Opry. He always made me laugh!

It was always special when I was able to play the Opry with my first producer, Brent Rowan.

Below: Taking a picture with Tony Perkins from my first appearance on *Good Morning America.*

Myles Mizukami

Roberts Family Archives

Myles Mizukami

Roberts Family Archives

Top right: Singing at the Dutchess County Fair.

Bottom right: On stage performing at the Taste of Chicago Festival.

I am celebrating with my touring band at my gold record party (left to right: Mickey Cones, me, Chris Autry, Danny Memeo, Frank Cuden).

I am posing on the red carpet at CMA Music Fest in Nashville, Tennessee (2017).

Below: Performing for my fan appreciation show in Nashville, Tennessee (2017).

Right: I am singing the national anthem at a Tennessee Titans NFL football game in Nashville (2013).

Robin Black

Mama and I won the TJ Martell Cake decorating contest in 2006. Our cake had a "Men and Mascara" theme.

Roberts Family Archives

Sitting with Mama on a porch swing at an event I was performing at in Nashville, Tennessee (2013).

Roberts Family Archives

I am sitting with MawMaw outside a Cracker Barrel in South Carolina on one of my visits back home (2018).

I am with Shooter Jennings outside the studio in Los Angeles with all the musicians who played on my album produced by Shooter (left to right: Ted Russell Camp, Jamie Douglas, me, Shooter Jennings, Neal Casal).

Left: Shooter and me celebrating after we finished recording my new album (2017).

Below: I am standing outside the bus Shooter and I were traveling on with the band (2017).

I am proudly wearing the green band jacket Jessi Colter let me borrow from her closet.

Right: Mama and me at the beginning of the 50 Mile Challenge walk for the National MS Society in Charleston, South Carolina (2015).

Below: On the red carpet for a National MS Society Fundraiser event I was speaking and performing at in Cleveland, Ohio (2018).

Roberts Family Archives

Roberts Family Archives

Guess what? I'm not a runaway bride after all! I found my soulmate and married him on June 23, 2018.

Sara Krauss

18

Not Again!

Tennessee is known as "the Volunteer State," and it is a nickname well deserved. A number of volunteers—including people from Mercury, my now former record company—showed up to help Mama and me get back on our feet. The kindness of friends and strangers was our lifeline.

A friend with whom I worked out knew about a furnished condo owned by a young woman planning to get married. The condo was for sale, but she graciously allowed us to live there for a few weeks until we could find somewhere else. We hadn't realized what a blessing it was simply to have an address.

The doorbell rang one morning, and a UPS driver delivered several boxes of clothes, towels, and personal items sent from people in South Carolina. I was overwhelmed with emotion as I saw the generosity of friends and family from our home area. We needed everything they sent.

Another friend, Jessie Roesch, who worked as a nanny for two of the young women who sang with the Christian singing group Point of Grace, allowed us to borrow her car. That was a tremendous blessing, as well, especially since we needed to travel back and forth to our house, and Mama had to go back to work.

We lived in four different places following the flood and still had a mortgage payment, even though we couldn't live in our house. "Isn't there any grace in this sort of situation?" Mama asked our banker. "Do I still have to make the house payments?"

"Yes," he said. "We can waive your payments for a couple of months and then tack them on to the end of the mortgage, but you will have to pay double interest on those delayed payments."

"Never mind," Mama said. "I don't want to extend our mortgage. We'll make it somehow."

In the immediate aftermath of the flood, a Nashville music publicist arranged for me to do several "live from the Cumberland River" television interviews with popular meteorologist Jim Cantori of the Weather Channel. Hobbling around on a broken ankle, I was giving so many flood updates I thought I might get a job as the network's newest weather girl!

Later, I did an interview on *Good Morning America* in which Robin Roberts came to Nashville and did a feature on me. We did a walk-through with me in our flood-trashed home, as we were cleaning crud and getting ready for the rebuilding process. Robin had me retell the story of our experiences during the flood, how we had to be rescued from the second floor of our townhome, and how we had lost everything to the swirling, muddy waters.

Bruton Smith saw the feature and called me the next morning. I was surprised to hear from him. "Is your insurance going to cover the damages?" he asked.

"No, we don't have flood insurance," I told him.

"Oh, that's too bad," Bruton said. "Why don't you let me buy you a house, and then you can pay me for it."

That was a tempting offer, but after the awkward situation I had experienced at his home in LA, I didn't think it was wise to allow Bruton to purchase us a new home.

"We'll be okay," I told him. "But I appreciate your kind offer."

Since we had no flood insurance—few people in our neighborhood did—we were on our own when it came to gutting, cleaning, and paying for the rebuilding of our home.

Our first chore was to pull up the muddy carpet and drag it out to the street in front of our house. Everything had to go. Then came the job of ripping off all the drywall that had gotten wet and was prone to developing black mold. All of that, too, had to be dragged out to the streets, awaiting removal. Entire families' most treasured possessions were stacked in huge piles of debris along the streets.

Luke Lewis called to see how we were, and he sounded sincerely concerned. I was still devastated over the demise of my record deal, but I appreciated his compassion nonetheless. As a board member of the Nashville-based MusiCares organization, an industry-wide humanitarian effort to help people in times of need, Luke encouraged MusiCares to help us. Luke allowed a number of people from Universal Music Group to take off work so they could put on work clothes and come help Mama and me clean muck from our home.

Even the upstairs flooring and walls were spattered with mud, but some of our clothes in closets and drawers seemed salvageable. Because we weren't sure whether our house would be condemned and torn down, we needed to quickly pack up anything we wanted to keep and take it to a storage unit. The Mercury staff helped me go through all our clothing that could be cleaned, stuff it into white garbage bags, and toss it out the windows, where it could be loaded into a van. I appreciated their help so much, yet it was humbling and demeaning to have people I didn't even know packing up our possessions going through my drawers, and handling my underwear, bathroom products, and other personal items. Over the coming months, I grew to despise the storage unit that held the remains of our decimated lives.

A number of our friends pitched in to help us tear out our carpet, flooring, and walls, stripping the house down to its studs. Church groups brought sandwiches and water to us as we worked. The kindness and generosity of Christian people toward us, and so many other people in our neighborhood, were amazing.

Pulling up carpet one day, I noticed that my hands were getting weak and numb. At first, I tried to ignore it, thinking that I was merely overly tired, suffering the effects of fatigue, but before long, I could not even lift a hammer or a crowbar.

Then my vision blurred.

These were the same symptoms I had experienced when I was first diagnosed with MS. Apparently, the stress of losing the movie, losing my record deal, and finally losing my home, car, and most of my possessions had exacerbated the MS.

I had thought the MS had gone away. It had been more than five years since I had been diagnosed, and throughout most of that period, the symptoms had remained dormant. As far as I knew, I was doing fine—until now.

"God, what is going on here? What do you want me to do?" I prayed aloud. "Whatever it is, I'll do it."

At Mama's insistence, I went back to the neurologist who had first diagnosed me with MS. I admitted to him, "I never read any of your literature when I was here five years ago. I took it home and put it in a drawer. It's probably floating somewhere in the Harpeth River now." I shook my head with regret. "But I'm ready to accept the fact that I have MS and to do whatever I have to do to beat this thing. I want to live my dreams. I don't want this illness to stop me."

The doctor listened silently as I continued. "I feel that I have been saved for a reason, and there's something else I am supposed to do," I said. "I want to live with MS and show other people how they can do that too." I swallowed hard. "I'm sorry I didn't listen to you earlier, and I hope you aren't mad at me."

Beauty in the Breakdown

"I'm not mad at you," the doctor answered kindly. "Sometimes it takes a while for someone with MS to come to grips with it."

He ordered an immediate MRI that revealed, as we had guessed, the MS had not gone away but had, in fact, gotten worse. The MRI showed definitively that during the five-year period in which I had lived in denial, the MS progressed, causing many new lesions in my brain. That meant the immune cells within my body were vigorously attacking the myelin coating the nerve fibers in my brain. Even though I could not feel any pain or anything unusual until the symptoms showed up, the MS was active. If the lesions moved down my spinal cord, there was a chance I would no longer be able to walk. That was a frightening thought to me.

"You need to start therapy right now," the doctor instructed. "I don't think it is too late. This may be your last chance to slow down the disease." That was definitely a wake-up call for me. Visions of Carol once again flooded my mind. I recalled that she could not control the effects of the disease. With my doctor's help—and with God's—I was determined to do everything possible to overcome the further progression of the MS. There were no guarantees, but I felt that the doctor, God, and I made a great team.

The doctor put me on a strict disease-modifying therapy regimen. "There is no cure for MS—at least, not yet," he told me, "but the medication will help you live a normal life and hopefully inhibit the disease's progression."

"I'm ready," I said. "I want to live. I want to sing. I want to help some other people. Whatever it takes to help me do that, I'm willing."

186

One thing I knew I needed to do was go public. I wrote a blog to my fans, for the first time admitting that I had MS. I knew that I needed to acknowledge that I had been saved for a reason, not simply for country music or even for myself, but to share a message of hope with others who were hurting like Carol and like me.

With my as yet limited knowledge, I tried to explain to my fans that there is no root cause to MS, so we may never know how I developed it. The National MS Society says, "Some researchers theorize that MS develops because a person is born with a genetic predisposition to react to some environmental agent that, upon exposure, triggers an immune-mediated response." Vitamin D is a factor, and tobacco usage exacerbates the symptoms. I was going to start taking more vitamin D, and I didn't use tobacco. I told my fans honestly that I had no idea how this would affect my voice but that I was going to sing till I breathed my last.

I was not about to let MS define me. As is often said about other strongholds, I had MS, but I was not going to allow MS to have me. The biggest obvious drawback I was experiencing was the weakness in my hands and the constant fatigue. I asked my fans to pray for me, and I promised them that I'd be on the road again, coming to sing for them soon.

Many of my fans wrote me encouraging cards and letters, and everyone I heard from was sympathetic and inspiring. Of course, because I went public, most people in the Nashville music industry were also now aware that I had MS. But other than my friend Erin, who was still working in Luke's office, not a single person in the music industry called, texted, sent a card, or offered any sort of encouragement at all. Although nobody would admit it, I later learned that many people believed the revelation that I had MS spelled doom for my music career. They simply didn't know what to say or how to console me.

It would be nearly a year and a half before I heard from anyone in the music business. Ironically, when somebody in music finally reached out to me, it would be a voice from the past that I least suspected.

19

Starting Over

Once all the sludge from the flood was removed from our house, Mama's friend Bob acted as our general contractor to guide us through the rebuilding process.

MusiCares offered to help pay for an apartment until we could complete the reconstruction process, so we moved into an apartment in Franklin for nearly six months while our home was being gutted, cleaned, and rebuilt. We had no furniture in the apartment, so we sat on the floor until some friends gave us some basic items.

Mama received an insurance settlement check for her destroyed car and was able to purchase a new vehicle, but for some reason, my car insurance settlement was slow in coming.

When Bruton Smith learned that I had no vehicle of my own, he called one of his dealerships and told them, "Julie hasn't received her car insurance settlement yet, so can you allow her to have a loaner until her money comes?"

The dealer responded to Bruton immediately and gave me a car to drive, rent free. It said LOANER in large letters on the back of it, but I didn't mind. It was a vehicle.

Of course, along with Bruton's kindness came . . . well, Bruton. He called often. "When you gonna come see me, honey?" he asked.

"I can't come," I told him. "We have a lot of work to do here, Bruton." At one point, in exasperation, I responded brusquely, almost rudely, with him on the phone. Shortly after that, somebody came by where we were living and picked up the car that Bruton's dealership had allowed me to use.

It was the end of December 2010 before we were finally able to get back into our home. We put up a Christmas tree to celebrate, even though we had no furniture. Denise Jones, from Point of Grace, and her husband, Stu, gave us a dining room table; someone else gave us a living room chair. Little by little, our piecemeal décor took shape.

It was both deeply moving and deeply humbling to have to accept these gifts from kind and generous friends. I had always enjoyed giving, and it was difficult for me to receive. It hurt my pride. But I was realizing more and more that as I was willing to humble myself, God would not only bless me but also use me in ways I had never even dreamed.

⌒

I immersed myself in work, writing and recording new songs and performing concert dates around the country that I booked myself. I came home off the road one day and found a beautiful, formal invitation addressed to Mama and me. I hurried to open it and, to my surprise, discovered an invitation to a party in honor of Luke Lewis for his many years and accomplishments with Universal Music Group. Since I had left UMG, I was pleasantly surprised that we would be invited to such an exclusive event.

Mama and I couldn't have been more excited. It was as if we'd been invited to Prince William's wedding! For a week, all we could talk about was what we were going to wear and how much weight we needed to lose to look fabulous in our dresses. Mama and I could be such *girls* when it came to parties.

Whether Luke realized it or not, I regarded him during my time at Mercury as my Nashville dad. Just as a dad would do for his own child, Luke tried his best to make my dreams come true, so despite my ignominious departure from the label, I still held Luke in the highest regard.

But I wasn't sure Luke knew that. We had talked only briefly in the aftermath of the Nashville flood, when he had called to see how I was doing.

As I got ready for the gala in Luke's honor, I had butterflies in my stomach, and it felt as though they were playing hockey in there! I hadn't seen Luke in a couple of years. *What will we say to each other? Will he be excited to see me?* I wondered. I had always loved the fact that Luke had been able to see me as more than his assistant, but would he still regard me that way? Or would he be cool and aloof, standoffish or distant, perhaps feeling somewhat guilty about what he had allowed to happen to my career and our friendship? I didn't really know.

From the moment Mama and I entered the room, it was like a family reunion. I saw so many people with whom I had worked closely at Mercury. I spotted a number of other music artists there, as well, including Kathy Mattea, Laura Bell Bundy, Lee Ann Womack, and the guys from Rascal Flatts. Everyone we talked with was so kind and friendly.

We moved through the crowd, talking with old friends and meeting a few new. Various executives from UMG stood and told stories about Luke and heaped accolades upon him, noting his many achievements in the business. And then it was time for Luke to say a few words. He thanked everyone for coming and mentioned a few highlights from his long career at UMG. He then looked around the room slowly, as if noting each person. "If you are here tonight, it is because I love you and wanted you here," Luke said, his voice quivering with emotion.

When Luke said those words, it was as though I was the only person in the room, and he was saying them directly to me. All the nervousness and anxiety about seeing him again melted away.

As soon as Luke was done with his speech, I walked over to him and hugged him. "I am so excited for you on your new journey," I said. I looked him in the eyes as I spoke to him. "Luke, I love you and appreciate everything you ever did for me. Thank you."

"I love you, too, Julie," he said, "and I'm sorry I missed your show in Nashville a few weeks ago."

"Don't worry about that," I said. "I'm sure you were busy."

Luke paused, as though he was going to say something and then thought better of it. He looked at me with tenderness in his face. "Don't you ever give up, girl. You've got it. Don't you ever quit!"

I could feel tears beginning to well in my eyes as I looked back at this man who had believed in me enough to give me a chance. I hugged him one more time and said, "I'm not giving up, Luke. I'm not. Now go enjoy your party!"

I smiled from the inside out as I watched him move through the crowd. I had a feeling that Luke and I would be seeing each other again.

When I lost my record deal, I also lost my booking agent and my PR team from Mercury. I had been with Creative Artists Agency, one of the most prestigious entertainment and sports agencies in the world, for more than five years. They wielded a lot of clout and could book me in venues I was unable to access on my own. But since the flood, I had been trying to book dates, secure media attention, and arrange travel details all by myself.

My longtime manager, Ron Shapiro, was gone too. I loved Ron and respected his opinions, but there came a point that it did not make financial sense for Ron to manage me remotely from New York. I could no longer afford to pay him, and although he was willing and gracious to do as much as possible for free, after the flood, I couldn't really even afford his travel expenses to and from Music City for meetings. "I think you need to find somebody in Nashville," he said, "who can work more closely with you."

Ron had reached out by phone in negotiations with Luke Lewis about moving forward with my next album, but Luke seemed entrenched in his position that without the Lifetime movie, Mercury was done with me. Ron had run Atlantic Records, so he understood the formidable obstacles Luke faced regarding my place on his label.

Ron and I parted ways professionally but remained friends.

In Nashville one day, I bumped into my friend Tim, with whom I had formerly worked in the Universal Music Group mailroom. Since our humble beginnings, Tim had moved up in his career and was now an assistant to Reen, a Universal artist and repertoire person who worked with pop groups out of her New York office but also maintained an office at UMG Nashville. When I told Tim that I was looking for new management to jump-start my career, he said, "Maybe you ought to talk with Reen. She's always liked you, and although she works for UMG, she is in a completely separate division from Luke. She might have some good advice for you."

I remembered Reen. I had known her since I was an intern at Universal Music Group. She impressed me because she was kind and spoke to the interns, something that many executives or other people in authority rarely did.

But Reen wasn't like that. She took an interest in helping the young, ambitious men and women on the lower echelons of the business and the younger employees in the company. She had always been friendly to me, even when I was a fledgling receptionist sitting outside Luke's office.

Tim offered to set up a lunch appointment with Reen. It was an informal meeting in which I felt comfortable asking for her opinions. I told her that I was no longer working with Luke. "What do you think I should do next?"

"Are you still working with Ron?" she asked.

"No, I'm looking for someone here."

"Well, I'd like to help you," Reen said. Universal had a relationship with Scott Borchetta's new label, Big Machine, that was changing the face of country music with his primary artist, Taylor Swift. Reen felt there might be an opening for me there. "I can get your record deal right back," Reen said.

"Really?" I asked, wide-eyed.

"Oh, yes. It may not be with Luke. It might be with Scott or someone else, but that shouldn't be a problem."

I was thrilled at the news and buoyed by her confidence. I signed with her on the rebound, looking for security rather than floundering by myself in the rough waters of the Nashville music business without Ron as my lifeboat.

After the flood, Reen became my manager, even though she worked for Universal. She fired my business manager without my knowledge, set up a new bank account for me, and began offering advice more regularly. But some of Reen's advice seemed odd to me. "You need to move out and not be living with your mother," she said. "It doesn't look right that a woman your age is still living with her mom."

That didn't sit right with me. Mama had sacrificed everything for me; I wasn't going to run out on her now that she was struggling to survive financially after the flood.

Reen also suggested that I go out with a rowdy female artist who had hit the news for smoking weed and being drunk at a show in Nashville. "That's the kind of stuff you need to be doing," Reen said. "To get some instant attention."

I knew that Reen was right in one sense. Those kinds of stories show up in tabloids every day. But that wasn't the kind of attention I wanted. Not surprisingly, Reen and I soon parted ways.

One of the best things that Reen did for me, however, was to reconnect me with Brent Rowan. Since I had been preparing to record my third full-blown album for Mercury, I had been writing with Marcus Hummon and other established Nashville songwriters. Reen felt—and I agreed with her— that I needed to return to my roots and get back to making music the way I had with Brent.

The only problem, of course, was that I had not seen or talked with Brent since 2005, more than six years earlier. "Let me work on that," Reen said.

Reen contacted Brent and arranged a meeting at his home studio. I was nervous as I drove into the expensive-looking gated community where Brent now lived, but I was super excited to see him. I pulled into his circular driveway, and Brent greeted me warmly at the front door of his house. Thanks to his easygoing manner, my sense of awkwardness and anxiety dissipated instantly. Brent showed me around his impressive home studio, complete with all the bells and whistles of any state-of-the-art studio on Music Row. However, Brent's studio included something I had not seen in any other facility. A devout Christian, Brent had built a chapel in the studio.

As we talked, I realized that nobody had ever told him the truth about our artistic breakup. So I told him everything. This was the first time Brent had heard the full story of how our professional recording deal with Mercury had dissolved. It was also the first that Brent discovered that it had not been *my* decision to change producers.

He told me that nobody from the record label had ever communicated that to him, and I admitted that I did not know that Brent had not been properly informed. We talked and cried, and I apologized to Brent for hurting him.

Brent graciously accepted my apology.

Eventually, we got around to talking about my future recording plans, and I asked him if he would be willing to work with me again.

"I need to talk with my wife about that," he said. I realized that the blowup with Mercury had not only affected Brent professionally and financially, but it had also affected him on an intensely personal level. His wife, Jill, knew that better than anybody, so I understood that he would want to discuss the possibility of our working together with her.

That was the type of relationship that Brent and Jill had, and I admired them as a married couple.

We parted that day with a hug, and it felt good that the air had finally been cleared between us, whether we ever were able to work together professionally or not.

Reen followed up and asked Brent to begin working with me on a speculative basis—doing the work first and then hoping to reap a reward. Producers of his stature rarely had the time or desire to do that, and in our conversation, I had explained to Brent that I didn't have the money to pay him in advance. So the chances of us working together were slim.

Nevertheless, a week or so later, we recorded a guitar and vocal of the song "Alive," written by some of Nashville's most prolific hit songwriters, Craig Wiseman, Steve McEwen, and Tom Douglas. Reen said, "Just record a couple of demos, and I will pitch them to some labels and get you a deal."

Whether she did or not, I may never know. When nothing tangible came of her efforts, I didn't feel that I could ask Brent to continue working on spec with no guarantee of future compensation to produce my new album. I was sad, but not discouraged.

During this time, a verse of Scripture that I had learned as a child really began to speak to me: "'For I know the plans I have for you,' declares the LORD, 'plans to prosper you and not to harm you, plans to give you hope and a future,'" (Jeremiah 29:11). I posted the verse everywhere: on my computer, on my website, and on my "vision board," a board on which I kept my goals in front of me, where I could see them every day.

More importantly, despite the setbacks I had experienced, that verse helped me to believe that God had good things in store for me, and that he was going to use the calamities that had come my way for his glory and for my good. I understood that I had to do my part, to work hard and keep pushing on doors till something opened. That meant I had to humble myself and be willing to do some things that weren't considered cool in the music business.

I had been mulling over my next moves regarding my recording career, and had already written a number of songs with top Nashville songwriters Marcus Hummon, Victoria Banks, Tom Douglas, Darrell Scott, and Chris Stapleton, as well as Don Schlitz. I was ready to get started on my third album, even if that meant producing an independent record on my own.

Reen suggested that I talk with Jason Collum, my drummer and bandleader. "He and his brother have a production company," Reen said, "and they might be able to help you somehow." Although Jason had been working with me for several years, I really had not known him outside of the band prior to the Nashville flood. We had worked on songs and arrangements together and had even gone out to eat alone the night before the flood, but our relationship had been mostly on a professional level.

On a long flight to Australia, where we were traveling to perform a USO show for the troops, Jason and I struck up a conversation about his production company. "We work mostly with film and television," he said, "placing songs in movies and TV shows, but we also record a lot of music." I was intrigued by Jason's projects, but he didn't push his outside business on me, which I appreciated.

I asked Jason if he would help me, and he agreed to coproduce the record with me and absorb some of the recording studio costs. We still needed money to pay musicians and other basic manufacturing costs when the album was done.

About that time, I finally received the delayed settlement from my insurance, reimbursing me for the loss of my car. Rather than using my car insurance settlement to purchase a new car, I decided to use the money to help finance the new album. My fans hadn't heard anything from me since *Men and Mascara*, and now that I had lost my record deal, I would not be recording the remaining five albums for Mercury. So I felt that I needed to record a new project on my own label that I called Ain't Skeered Records, the same name I had labeled my touring company. I called the album *Alive*, because I wanted the world to know that I was still alive; I had been saved in more ways than one.

As we were working on the album, Bruton Smith called to check how Mama and I were doing. He knew that I was struggling, and I sincerely appreciated his concern. "Just tell me, honey," he'd say again and again. "What can I do to help?"

This time, I had something in mind. "Bruton, I want to record a song that NASCAR might be able to use as a theme song. We can do a video of the song and feature all your racetracks."

I had written a song, "NASCAR Party," along with Nick Trevisick and Thom Hardwell, to pitch to NASCAR. Hank Williams Jr.'s song "All My Rowdy Friends Are Here on Monday Night" had been used as the opening theme for Monday Night Football on ABC-TV for more than two decades. I knew that the stock car racing giant did not have anything similar. Yet they were packing thousands of fans into racetracks all year long, with millions more watching on television every week.

Bruton sent the song to the NASCAR top brass, and they arranged to pay for the production of the video. The video had it all—action scenes from races at tracks all over the country, some top drivers, fans having fun, plenty of food and drink—and of course, me singing and dancing. We filmed much of it at Texas Motor Speedway and at Charlotte Motor Speedway. In a couple of scenes, I'm even sitting behind the wheel of one of the race cars. And yes, we got a shot of Bruton in the video!

The video was great fun to make, but unfortunately, due to personnel changes within NASCAR, we were not able to close the deal. I was disappointed, and it didn't make sense to me. NASCAR had invested a lot of money in the recording and video project. The video still can be found on YouTube. It wasn't a wasted effort, though, since I included "NASCAR Party" on my *Alive* album, and it became one of my fans' most requested songs.

With the *Alive* album done, my next goal was to secure a new booking agent and management company. In the meantime, I worked every day to get my new album out to radio stations and to the public. I packed up orders and took them to the post office to mail.

Jason Collum's company had an advisory board composed of significant Nashville movers and shakers. One of the members of the board was Joe Galante, former head of RCA in Nashville. I met with Joe and told him about my experiences with Luke, the flood, and my recent efforts to reestablish my career. He suggested that I sign with a boutique agency to help me promote my independent project.

"I like Tony Conway," Joe said. "I'll reach out to him and ask him to meet with you." Tony had worked for years with Buddy Lee Attractions, one of the long-standing premier talent agencies in Nashville.

I met with Tony about booking me, and we got along so well, we decided he should be my manager as well. Tony was smart and knowledgeable about the business, and I knew instinctively that I could trust him. His was a family business at the time, and I got to know his wife and daughter too. I don't know if they adopted me as part of their family, but I adopted them as mine.

Tony booked some great concert dates for me, and that was helpful. Even more so, Tony piqued my imagination of what could be. One of Tony's strong suits was long-term planning. He and I had numerous meetings in which he would fill a whiteboard with potential ideas for me. I loved thinking about where I wanted to go and how I might get there, so I always left Tony's office inspired, whether our ideas came to fruition or not.

It was during one of those motivational meetings when Tony broached an unusual idea to me, one that might be a game changer.

20

The Voice

In late summer 2012, I was approached by television producers to appear on the NBC-TV reality show *The Voice*. I turned it down because I was busy promoting my recent self-released album, *Alive*. But after I signed with Tony Conway to manage and book me, Tony and I revisited my decision.

"I don't know, Tony," I fretted. "It feels like a step backward. That show is known mostly for featuring unknown artists, which is great for singers who are just starting out or have never had a record contract. I don't fit into either of those categories."

"It's a lot of television exposure," he countered. "Appearing on *The Voice* might be great for you, Julie."

Eventually Tony convinced me to give it a try. The fourth

season of *The Voice* was scheduled to tape in Burbank in the fall of 2012, and I signed a contract agreeing to do the show.

Tony and I thought I had nothing to lose. We could not have been more wrong.

⟶

I was sad as I packed for Los Angeles and prepared to leave Mama and our dogs. The last few years had been hard on her as we both tried to rebuild our broken lives.

I left Mama a couple of cards to express my thanks to her and to lift her spirits. I wrote "Open After I Leave" on the envelope. Inside a card depicting a cute little dog with the words "Thank You" on the front, I wrote:

Mama,

I wanted to let you know how much I appreciate every single thing you do for me! I am so blessed to have you in my life . . . please take care of yourself for me. Try not to worry so much, and also sleep, exercise, and eat healthy!

In another card depicting a pretty dog, I wrote:

Mama,

By the time you open this, I will be on my journey. I am going to work really hard so I can take care of you again. Thank you for helping me decide this was the right path for me to take at this time. I believe with all my heart that great things are about to come our way.

I hope that by the time you read this I am so busy I don't have time to be sad, because I sure am sad writing this card. I love you so much and will miss you so much. I will call as often as possible. Take care of yourself and have some fun while I'm gone!

Thanks for watching the sweet puppies. I hope they stay well for you. I love you, Mama!

Julie

The premise of *The Voice* is that talented singers audition in front of an audience and four judges known for their success in the music business. Nothing is new about that, but on *The Voice*, the judges are faced toward the audience while the singer performs. That's why this early stage of the competition is known as the blind auditions. Each judge has a button that reads "I Want You" that can be pressed at any time during the performance, indicating that the judge wants that singer on his or her team for the remainder of the competition. In later stages of the show, the judge becomes that singer's coach, in competition with the singers chosen by the other three coaches. If two or more judges press their buttons and turn around, then the singer must decide which judge will be the best coach to further him or her in the competition. If none of the coaches turn around during the performance, then that singer is eliminated from the competition and is sent home. The winning contestant receives a monetary prize of $100,000 and a recording contract with Universal Music Group.

Ever since I was a little girl on the competition circuit, I'd known that song choice was crucial. I was at my best when I could relate to a song's lyrics and make the performance my own. I worried that picking the wrong song for my blind audition would end my time on the show before it even got started. I had one shot to wow the judges, and I had to make it count.

Of course, you can't go on a televised reality show and sing anything you want. Music publishers see shows like *The Voice* as a lucrative money-making opportunity, and some publishers don't allow certain songs in their catalogs to be used without enormous financial payments. I was limited to whatever songs had already been cleared for use.

Unfortunately, none of the songs I'd hoped to sing were in the clear. Tony was confident that I could make any song my own, but I just couldn't seem to land on something that was a good fit.

I felt defeated, and I hadn't even sung a note. *Maybe this was a mistake*, I thought.

The Blake Shelton song "God Gave Me You," originally written and recorded by Dave Barnes, was the least pop-sounding song of the ones that had been cleared. If I could follow Dave's original lead rather than Blake's, I stood a chance of performing it in my own style. So I went to work learning the Dave Barnes version of "God Gave Me You," perfecting not only the notes themselves but the gestures and stage presence to go along with them.

The morning of my blind audition, I met the staff downstairs in the hotel at ten o'clock, and they ushered me to the studio where I was to perform for the judges and audience. I waited anxiously, walking the halls, focusing on all that my vocal coach had suggested, especially that I sing to the audience rather than to the judges in the chairs. I wore a bright red, high-necked dress with a black belt, a comfortable outfit that I had picked out myself. I accessorized with a gold cross, large circular "diamond" earrings, and heels, and was fully made up backstage.

I knew that Mama was in a room nearby waiting, but I was not permitted to see her or communicate with her. The only time I saw her was when Carson Daly did an interview with her and me as part of the package that would air before my performance.

The production assistants checked me over, making sure that everything was exactly the way it was supposed to be, right down to my earrings.

It was close to four o'clock before the producers called for me. I walked into the backstage area, where one of the main producers welcomed me. It was finally my turn to sing. The film crew stopped, as the cameras, lights, and microphones were repositioned as necessary after the previous contestant's performance. "Please take your places," the director called.

A production assistant ushered me out to the spot onstage they had previously indicated, where I was supposed to stand when I began singing. That was no surprise to me, since I'd performed on television a number of times. I knew that very little about TV is actually spontaneous. "Stand here, turn your head this way, look at that camera."

The judges—Blake Shelton, Shakira, Adam Levine, and Usher—faced away from me and toward the audience as the lights came up on me.

I moved to the end of the stage and attempted to sing to the audience, although most of them already had their favorites, since the audience was mostly composed of guests invited by the contestants. Still, I knew that a positive reaction from the crowd could sway the judges' opinions.

As I sang, I kept waiting for Blake Shelton to turn around. When I got to the middle of the performance, and still none of the judges had turned around, I started to worry. *Will anybody pick me?*

My entire performance took barely more than one minute. As I held out the last note, not one judge had turned around.

Despite my worry over the song choice, I hadn't really considered that I might not make it past the blind audition. Of all the ways I had imagined my time on *The Voice* going down, this wasn't one of them.

I was crushed. I felt like bursting into tears. But I knew I had to be strong, so I continued smiling and held my head high as I thanked the audience.

The judges finally did turn around, all four of them at once. Blake looked surprised but not shocked.

"Oh!" he said. "Ohhh! Oh, I know her," Blake said as he leaned forward and put his hand over his eyes. "Oh, man, and she sang my song." Blake raised up and said, "This is Julie Roberts, everybody, by the way." The crowd applauded in response.

"Honestly," Blake attempted to explain, "because I know all the ins and outs of that song, and you took it and did your own thing with it. And I should have known that was you. Dadgumit. I'm sorry; I'm so sorry." Blake looked to Usher and said, "Say something, Usher."

Usher did not seem to know me, but he was kind. "This is a great opportunity for you to share your talent with the rest of the world," he said. "Continue to be passionate about what you do."

"I am," I said. It struck me that Usher was simply trying to put a positive spin on a disaster, so I reciprocated in a similar manner. "I'm definitely not stopping now."

"I hope not!" Usher responded, nodding and smiling. "I hope not."

"Thank you all so much for listening," I said before exiting the stage. The words sounded surreal to me. I heard myself saying them, but I was in a daze. I felt as though I had been suddenly thrust backward in time to one of those beauty pageants in which I'd competed as a child.

"Thank you, Julie," Blake called, beginning the applause.

"Thank you, Blake," I said with a wave.

In the follow-up interview, Blake said, "Julie Roberts came out here and I'm still sick to my stomach over this. She just kinda fell through the cracks in the business . . . I'm so sorry I didn't turn my chair around."

Maybe so, but he had not responded, nor had any of the other judges, so I was eliminated from the competition.

I replayed the performance over and over in my mind, trying to figure out what I had done wrong. Maybe my discomfort with the song arrangement had shown through after all, but I had picked the song I felt I could do the best with. Nevertheless, I couldn't help thinking, *I just ruined my career and destroyed my life.*

I was so stressed and discouraged. I had been knocked down so many times before and had always gotten back up.

But I wondered if my heart could take another devastating blow.

Mama worried that I might have a nervous breakdown, or worse yet, an MS relapse, because I was so upset. "Mama, we've survived much worse than this," I said, trying to dispel her fears. Still, I couldn't wait to get out of there.

I returned to Nashville, and for days, I didn't even want to get out of bed. I certainly didn't want to face my friends or anybody in the music business. I had been convinced that my appearance on *The Voice* was going to be my reintroduction to the music world. Instead, the way it played out plunged me into prolonged, deep despair. Over the next few months, I prayed again and again, *God, did I do something wrong? Am I being punished? I know you hear me. Please help me see the purpose in all of this.*

The episode including me on *The Voice* aired—appropriately for me—on April Fools' Day. I watched it along with millions of other people, seeing for the first time the preperformance package about my story of rising from the receptionist to the recording artist, to losing it all after being diagnosed with MS, and then losing my record deal and my home.

Then came my song. The worst part to me was watching the sad expression on Mama's face as she held out hope to the very last note that one of the judges would respond to me.

That same evening, I put out a message to my fans. It

took me a while to write it because tears kept welling in my eyes.

As some of you may have seen tonight, I was one of the blind auditions featured on *The Voice*. I haven't been able to talk about my experience with *The Voice* until it aired and now that it has, I wanted you all to hear about it directly from me.

For the last two years, I have been invited to come audition to participate in the show, and this past year, I decided to take a chance and see what would happen if I did. So, I took the first step and went to Memphis, TN, last summer to meet with the producers and sing for them. Then, they invited me to move to LA for about 6 weeks to participate in the blind auditions.

While in LA, I met so many wonderful people including other contestants, my amazing vocal coach, and so many special folks that God brought into my life for that season.

Obviously, if you are reading this and watched the show, you know that a chair did not turn around for my blind audition. This was heartbreaking for me on many levels but I believe with all my heart that God has other plans for my life that he is working on behind the scenes for me right now.

I've been back from LA several months now and I am writing and recording music! In fact, I will be releasing new music for you very soon! I'm also working on booking some shows and getting out there on the road to you as well.

I am more motivated than ever to reach my musical and career goals! My plan is to always create and play music for all of you that I love so much!!!!

Thank You for your continued support and God Bless You!

My fans' reactions were mixed. "Why didn't you sing one of your songs?" many wanted to know. I couldn't tell them that the choice was not mine.

Others said, "I can't believe that Blake didn't turn around!" I couldn't answer for Blake. Others hinted that since Blake and Miranda Lambert were together as a couple by then, that perhaps he felt she would be jealous if he chose me. But that was silly. Miranda and I were friends.

Regardless of the reasons I was not chosen, appearing on *The Voice* was a horrible experience for me. I had willingly gone on the show, but then I was completely embarrassed and devastated when nobody selected me. Rejection is always tough, no matter how long we've done something. I thought, *Have I worked this hard . . . all for this?*

It was one of the most painful experiences of my life, but the lessons learned through my appearance on the show spurred me on in my career, as well as in my personal life. I had learned again that I had to choose to overcome adversity, and that when bad things happened, I had two choices: I could mope—which I allowed myself to do for a while—or I could believe that God would use even this experience for good in my life and in the lives of others. I chose the latter. Moreover, as a result of my story being broadcast, I began receiving all sorts of communications from people who were living with MS, who told me how much seeing me on the show had inspired them. It was a good reminder that my life belongs to God, and he is the one in charge. I was learning never to put my faith in people to change my circumstances, because God is in control.

And I was about to learn that lesson again.

21

Prisoner of Love

Writing songs with Marcus Hummon, a Grammy-Award-winning songwriter, was a fantastic experience in itself, but I received unexpected residual blessings as a result. Marcus and his wife, Becca Stevens, were active in Thistle Farms, a business and ministry Becca founded to help women coming out of human trafficking, prostitution, drugs, alcohol, or other addictions. Many of these women have spent time in prison, so getting a job is difficult for them when they are released. To help solve that problem, Thistle Farms developed products the women could make and sell, which gave these women an opportunity to be employed and to get a fresh start. Most importantly, the meaningful employment helped restore the women's dignity.

I had recorded Marcus's song "No Way Out" on my first album, and Marcus and I had been working together on new songs that I had hoped to present to Luke Lewis for my third album. During that time, Marcus told me about what he called the Magdalene Tour. He and his wife went to various prisons around the country to sing and speak to the inmates.

"Do you think you'd ever want to come with us to sing in the women's prison?" Marcus asked.

I had never done that, and it scared me a little, but I had told God that I would do anything for him. I wasn't going to back away from that commitment.

Shortly after that, I went along with Marcus and Becca, and some of the women from Thistle Farms, to a women's correctional facility. I dressed in jeans and multiple layers of sweatshirts, with no skin exposed. It was an ominous feeling as we checked in with the prison guards, turning over our purses, phones, identification—everything. We took nothing but our instruments through the security gates. Hearing those heavy steel-barred doors clank shut behind me was one of the scariest sounds I'd ever heard. Then we went through more barred doors until we were deep within the bowels of the prison.

The guards gathered the inmates into a room used as a chapel, and the chaplain introduced us. Marcus opened the program with his song "God Bless the Broken Road," and then I sang "No Way Out" and "I'll Fly Away," and a few other gospel songs. I was nervous until I started singing, and then the music broke down the barriers. Some of the women even sang along with me.

As I looked into the faces of the women, some of whom looked really tough, I thought, *With a few wrong choices, this could easily have been Mama or me.*

The women from Thistle Farms told their stories, offering the inmates hope in Jesus even in prison and letting the women know there was help available when they got out of prison. As they waved goodbye to us, a few of the inmates had tears in their eyes. I had tears in mine as well. I felt that I had been a part of something significant, something that mattered, something that had lasting value.

We traveled to prisons all over the country. In Florida, the prison had a dog-training program in which some of the inmates participated. For some it was part of their "employment," and for others it was part of their therapy. The inmates trained old greyhounds or other large dogs to be service dogs. I love dogs, so I was interested when someone asked me if I wanted to see the dog unit.

A guard opened the locked door to a sequestered, glassed-in area, and our group went inside. I became engrossed in playing with a big, old dog relaxing in the far corner of the unit. I leaned over and rubbed his belly, and I didn't notice that the other members of our group had all been buzzed out by the guard.

When I looked up, I realized that I was all alone in the room with the dogs and a group of rough-looking, hardened women inmates—inside a separately locked-down section of the prison.

I tried to mask my fear, but apparently I didn't do so well. A woman saw me and realized that I was isolated. She moved close to me and fastened a dog collar around her neck. She got right up in my face and with a low-pitched, husky tone in her voice said, "My name's Wolfie. Do you wanna play?"

Frightened, I said, "Baah" or some sound that was supposed to be "Bye!" and made a dash for the buzzer.

To me, the most unnerving correctional and mental institution that we visited was Rikers Island in New York City, where more than ten thousand inmates, both male and female, were incarcerated. Located on a small patch of land in the East River between the Bronx and Queens, the prison was only a few hundred feet away from the runways of LaGuardia International Airport.

Rikers had a reputation for the abuse of inmates by the guards, as well as assaults by inmates on the uniformed officers and civilians who worked at the facility. Indeed, many of the guards I saw wore heavy protective gear and helmets. I noticed a male guard with a grotesque scar on his face. "What happened there?" I asked, pointing to the scar.

"That's a souvenir from our last riot here," he said somberly.

The warden permitted us to do a presentation for the female inmates, but refused to let us near any of the males. We were escorted to a gymnasium packed with women, and when we walked in, they were out of control, yelling, arguing, and ready for a fight. I was terrified, my heart pounding and my eyes darting in every direction, alert for any misconduct as I steeled myself for what was certain to be an intense meeting.

"Hey, quiet down!" one of the guards yelled. "These

people are here from Tennessee to tell you about the Magdalene program." The women ignored the guard and continued talking. Finally, Marcus and I simply began playing and singing.

Amazingly, as soon as they noticed the music, the women calmed down. The noise abated, and most of the women listened attentively to the entire program.

More than anything I took away from these encounters, I realized that these incarcerated women weren't much different from me. They had made some bad decisions and were suffering the consequences.

We all have had our ups and downs—I'd certainly had mine—but they had chosen a path that had gotten them into trouble. When Mama and I talked about it, we agreed that had either of us lost control and responded angrily to Daddy's abuse, we might easily have made similar counterproductive decisions.

Still grasping at any passing train in hopes of getting my career back on track, I received an offer through Jason Collum and his brother Josh's company to record a project for Sun Records in Memphis. Founded by Sam Phillips, Sun was most famous for being the company to first record superstars Elvis Presley, Johnny Cash, Jerry Lee Lewis, and Roy Orbison. Who wouldn't be honored to record for a company with such an illustrious legacy?

At the time we were talking about doing a project together, Sun Records had faded from the limelight and was not really regarded as a major player in the music industry. My project would be its first significant album in more than thirty years, which promised to be a huge PR story.

By this point, Jason and I had spent much more time together. He was a great guy with a strong Christian background, and he was an incredibly talented musician. He could play almost any instrument he picked up, and he was a good songwriter too. Neither of us was dating anyone else, so it just felt natural that the two of us should become a dating couple. Ironically, because we were together so much, on the road, in the studio, and writing together, we rarely actually "dated." Only occasionally did we go out simply to have fun. Few people who saw us working onstage together ever guessed that my drummer and bandleader was also my boyfriend, but we were definitely a couple.

Consequently, when the Sun Records opportunity came along, I simply trusted Jason and Josh to make wise decisions. The caveat to the Sun deal was that Josh wanted to manage me, even though he had never managed an artist previously. But Josh and Jason had been good to Mama and me following the flood, so I wanted to do something to repay them for their kindness. Moreover, their company had access to a savvy advisory board, which meant I'd have an entire team of people to help me.

I talked to Tony Conway, who had been managing me and booking my dates, and I outlined the Sun opportunity with him. "I feel like I've been stagnant since the *Voice* incident, and I need to do something different," I said. "Josh's group seems to have access to some money, and they plan to vigorously promote the record."

Tony looked at me kindly. "If somebody is willing to do all that for you, then I would tell you not to stay here," he said. "I think you should take them up on it." I appreciated Tony's attitude, and I believed that he truly wanted the best for me, even though it would take money out of his pocket.

I signed with Sun Records without an attorney, since I didn't have enough money to afford good representation, and Jason and I started writing songs for an album we'd eventually title *Good Wine and Bad Decisions*. The title said it all. It was yet another thing I jumped into, hoping that it would save me.

When I was ready to record, I went to Josh to arrange the details with Sun.

"Okay, great," Josh said. "Get me some money together and we'll get moving."

"Some money? I thought that Sun was paying for the recording costs."

"Oh no," Josh said. "They aren't going to pay for this record. You are."

"What do you mean? Why not?" I was surprised and appalled that the record company was not planning to cover the initial costs as an advance against future royalties. That's the way the business works—usually.

"This is not a recording contract. It is a *licensing* agreement," he said. "You can use their name and they can use yours."

That was news to me. I thought we had an agreement

similar to the deal I'd had with Mercury, only on a smaller scale.

"Well, I can't afford to pay for the album," I told him. "How are we going to finance it?" I was more than frustrated; I was upset that I had allowed myself to get into such an unwise financial agreement and worried about how I was going to pay for everything.

Josh suggested crowdfunding the album. The way it works is simple: I put out a notice that I was inviting individuals or companies to become my "executive producers," by contributing money to help fund the album. In return, I would grant incentives commensurate with the amount contributed. For instance, if someone donated twenty-five dollars, I would send that person an advance, signed copy of the album. Others might want to contribute one hundred dollars or more, and they received more perks as my thanks. Other companies or individuals might want to visit in the studio while we were recording, or book me for a private event in return for a certain level of contribution. Pledge— the company that handled the crowdfunding—received a percentage of all the funds that were collected.

Since I had an established fan base, the idea seemed to make good financial sense. And my fans showed up big-time. They contributed enough that I could pay for the recording of the album, and we recorded some great music.

My agreement with Sun gave me access to its enormous song catalog. I found an old song, "He Made a Woman Out of Me," as recorded by Bobbie Gentry, the mysterious Grammy-Award-winning artist who had earned enormous success with the haunting, iconic ballad "Ode to Billy Joe."

I'd always loved Bobbie's voice and her songs, so that was an easy choice for me.

Vince Gill graciously lent his voice to a song on the album, as did Buddy Miller. I had recorded a couple of Buddy's songs on previous albums, and I was tickled to have his voice on my album. I wrote a number of the songs, and the album captured the soulful, bluesy sort of sound that I had done on my first album.

For distribution—getting the album out to retail outlets—we worked out an agreement with Sony RED, although the record still said Sun Records. That sounded like a good deal, but the devil was in the details. I paid for my own photo shoot, my own publicity, and even for the packaging and shipping of all the albums preordered by my fans. I packed albums on my living room floor, hauled them to the post office, and paid for the postage, all at my own expense. I also paid for the production of a video for the song "He Made a Woman Out of Me." Before long, I was wallowing in so much debt, I had to take out a loan to stay afloat.

That is not how the music business is supposed to work.

We debuted the album at my fan appreciation event held in Nashville during the 2013 Country Music Week in June. While I was onstage, talking about the album, a representative from Sun Records came up and talked about how excited they were to be working with me. "And we've brought along *Good Wine and Bad Decisions* / Sun Records T-shirts for everyone who has attended our release party today!" The crowd responded enthusiastically.

I thought it was so nice for Sun to do that—until I received a bill for more than $700 for the T-shirts that

I had not ordered or even known about until the onstage announcement.

Thankfully, other than the original agreement, I did not sign anything involved with the licensing part of the deal. That turned out to be a blessing. Because I had not personally signed the licensing contracts, when the term expired, I did not have to continue that relationship, so I didn't. This episode marked the beginning of a downhill slide in my relationship with Jason, as well, eventually leading to our breakup, although we remained friends and bandmates for quite a while.

What had started out as an exciting idea and a potentially great opportunity to promote my music turned out to be a disaster for which I'd be paying—literally—for many years. I did, however, come away from the experience with a lot more wisdom and some wonderful songs for which I own the publishing rights. The fans loved the album, I received some super reviews and great media responses, and I still sing many of the songs on that record to this day.

I had no intention of quitting. I chose to overcome any negative thoughts about the deal by believing that God would open another door. As I had since I was a child, I believed that my life was in his hands.

My faith has always been the cornerstone of my life. When we were kids, Mama took us girls to church as often as possible. We went to First Baptist Church's Sunday school, and I was involved in the children's and adult choirs. Mr. Barnes, a chipmunk-cheeked minister of music with a big, amazing operatic voice, led the choirs, and he often helped me with vocal techniques. For a while, I hoped that I could have chubby cheeks like Mr. Barnes because he was such a fabulous singer. I always accepted when Mr. Barnes offered me solos with the adult choir, and I especially enjoyed singing in the Easter and Christmas cantatas.

My favorite church activities revolved around a children's group called Girls in Action (GAs). Ms. Emmanuel, my teacher in GAs, had a brilliant method of getting her students to memorize Scripture. For each verse we memorized, she rewarded us with a miniature box of Butterfingers candy. I learned a bunch of Scripture, because I wanted those Butterfingers!

But it was the youth leader, Mr. Capps, who really connected with me and helped me to make sense of the Bible and what it meant to be a Christian. A kind, soft-spoken man, with dark hair and pale skin, Mr. Capps and his wife took an interest in me. His wife taught me basic piano lessons, and Mr. Capps taught me about what it meant to be "born again." He told me that Jesus loved me so much that he paid the price for my sins by dying on the cross.

I had never thought of my sins as being that serious. Oh, sure, Lorie and I sometimes got into mischief together, like the time we collected a bunch of Mama's cigarette butts and smoked them in our bedroom early in the morning. Mama came into our bedroom unexpectedly, and although she didn't see us smoking, the room reeked of smoke that was still hanging in the air.

"It's foggy this morning, ain't it, Mama?" I said.

Mama wasn't fooled for a moment. "Go pick out a switch," she said. "And make sure it's a good one." By a "good" switch, Mama meant a long, thin twig with plenty of flexibility. We were already shaking in fear long before we ever got back in the house and bent over to receive the swats with the switch. Those swats cured me of smoking forever. I never wanted to get spanked by Mama, mostly because I didn't want to disappoint her, but those switches stung plenty too!

On another occasion, Lorie and I let some stray cats inside the house and one of them got stuck in the La-Z-Boy. I didn't know it was there, so when I sat back in the chair, the mechanism trapped the cat and we couldn't get her out. The cat screeched and squealed, and we thought for sure it was going to die inside the back of that chair. In desperation, we called Mama at work and begged her to come home to rescue the cat, who eventually escaped unharmed. That cat may have had nine lives, but when Mama got home, I wasn't so sure about Lorie's and mine.

Despite our mischief, I never considered my sins as worthy of eternal damnation, but Mr. Capps reminded me that we've all fallen short of the glory of God, and we all needed to be forgiven. I talked with Mr. Capps about my relationship with Jesus, and when I was about twelve years old, we prayed together as I invited Christ to come into my life.

A few weeks later, when the pastor offered a challenge in the main Sunday service, I stepped out from where Mama, Marie, Lorie, and I were standing. I walked down to the front of the church, signifying that I was making a public commitment of my fledgling faith.

Pastor Roberts—who was no relation to us—baptized

Marie and me on the same morning in front of the entire congregation. Baptism was an important ceremony for me; I was making a public statement that I had decided to follow Jesus. Even at that young age, I had no illusions of being perfect, but I had talked to God every night from the time I was a child, and now that I understood more of who Jesus was and what he had done for me, I wanted to have a more intimate relationship with him.

Most of my closest friends already were or soon became Christians. They joined in the youth events at the Baptist or Methodist churches, and that positive peer pressure helped to keep us on the straight and narrow path when a lot of other kids were going in different directions.

Since that time, in a lot of ways, my life hadn't gone according to plan, but my faith in God remained strong. Here I was, at yet another crossroads. I had no idea what I was supposed to do in my career and in my life, but I believed that God would direct my steps and see me through. I prayed and longed for someone to come alongside me who believed in me and could help me fulfill God's plans for me. God must certainly have a fabulous sense of humor, because he answered that prayer in a most unusual way.

22

A "Voice" from the Past

I grew increasingly discouraged at my inability to make the right connections to get another record deal. It didn't make any sense. I was a proven entity in the music business. I had earned a gold record, had appeared on national television numerous times, and had played concerts all over the United States and in several European countries, but now I couldn't even get arrested, as the saying goes. I knew most of the major players in the Nashville music business, and most of them were kind to me, but I got the distinct impression that they now regarded me as damaged goods.

I prayed like never before. "God, I know I'm not finished. I want to get back out there and do what you have created me to do. Please help me."

The answer came in a somewhat surprising way.

I was driving down a road close to home one day, listening to "Outlaw Country" on satellite radio, when one of Waylon Jennings's songs came on my car radio. "Just some good ole boys," Waylon sang. I recognized it immediately as Waylon singing the theme song from the television show *Dukes of Hazzard*.

That's a "white truck" song, I said to myself, remembering our childhood trips to Mawmaw's house in Mama's white truck.

I smiled and pulled into a grocery store parking lot and listened to the entire song. While I was parked, I decided to check emails on my phone.

To my complete surprise, that same day, I had received an email from Shooter Jennings, the son of Waylon Jennings and Jessi Colter. I knew Shooter, but I hadn't had contact with him in more than ten years. The last time we had been together, we had played a date in Columbia, South Carolina. After that, Shooter sent me a song, "This Is Us," and wanted to record it together, but because we were both relatively new artists at the time, our labels refused to allow us to do it. We let the duet idea drop, but I held on to the song.

Now, ten years later, Shooter had contacted me on the same day I had heard his dad's song.

In his email, Shooter said, "Hey, I know that you've had a hard time since you told the industry that you have MS. But I believe in you, and I don't believe that you've had your best shot yet. I don't believe you have made your best record yet, and I want to help you." He signed it simply, "Shooter Jennings."

At first, I thought it was a joke. But then I remembered my prayer.

"Okay, God. This can't be merely a coincidence that I hear from Shooter the same day I hear his dad on my radio. And that he says he believes in me. I'm listening, God."

I sent a note back to Shooter, thanking him for his encouragement and his offer, but I was also completely honest with him. "I don't have any money. I can't afford to pay for you to produce a new record. I spent all my savings on a couple of independent projects on my own label, and I haven't made it back yet."

"If you can get to LA, I'll take care of the recording details," he said. "I'll be home for a few weeks, and I can book the studio. My sister, Julie, passed away recently, but before she died, she told me in the hospital, 'Shooter, I want you to record this song with a female artist.' And I thought of you."

"Really?" I was taken aback but pleasantly surprised. "Well, okay," I said. "But if I'm gonna come, why don't we also do that song, 'This Is Us,' that you sent to me ten years ago."

"You still have it?" Shooter sounded excited. "I forgot about that song!"

"Yeah, I do. One of the few things I could salvage from the flood was my laptop. It had all my songs on it, including the one you sent me."

"Wow, okay, bring it along. Now we'll get to do it!"

Hearing from Shooter was just the sort of encouragement that I needed. Music City had put me on a shelf. All I had left was Mama, my faith, my music, and my dogs. Having experienced so much loss and rejection in a relatively short period of time, my confidence was at an all-time low—not just my confidence in my musical ability but my confidence in *me*.

Shooter gave me some potential recording dates, so I got online and booked an inexpensive flight and an inexpensive hotel. I was excited to see him, but I had no idea what to expect. The idea that Shooter was a different breed of country artist appealed to me when I had first met him, and it intrigued me even more as I boarded a plane to LA to work with him in the recording studio.

Many people in the music business regarded Shooter Jennings as the epitome of his dad's "outlaw music mentality." Shooter didn't look, act, or sound like a country music artist. Although he was born into a country music family and grew up listening to George Jones, Johnny Cash, and Willie Nelson, Shooter is definitely a nonconformist. But then, so were his heroes—and mine. With his long, straight hair and grunge look, his demeanor and attitude said "rock and roll." Originally from Nashville, Shooter moved to Los Angeles in 2001 and worked with rock-oriented projects and bands. Yet his heart and roots were deeply entrenched in country music.

He sent me a note saying, "Don't feel pressure about doing a lot of music. I think starting with a tune or two will be good to see how you feel about working together."

Mama was unable to travel to California with me, so I invited my friend Kate Marshall to accompany me. Kate had never been in a recording studio and was fascinated by the possibility of meeting Shooter. Kate had loved the movie *Walk the Line*, in which Shooter had played his dad, so she convinced her husband, Lee, that I needed her with me—which I did! Mama was happy that Kate could go along too.

Kate and I flew in to LAX a day early to help us get acclimated. We met Shooter and his wife, Misty, at a restaurant bar the following evening for an informal get-together. It was the first time I'd seen Shooter in more than a decade, and he was just as friendly and welcoming as ever. Shooter was both a gentleman and a gentle man.

After about an hour, we walked to Shooter and Misty's townhouse nearby and talked for a long time about their kids and Shooter's mom, but very little about our plan for the recording session. I asked Shooter, "Shouldn't we talk about what key we're going to do the songs in and things like that?"

"Oh no," Shooter said. "My bandleader, Ted, is real good at that sort of thing, and he'll figure it all out when we get to the studio."

That was new to me. In Nashville, producers showed up at the studio with the song charts, keys, and everything else all printed out for the studio musicians. Not Shooter. He wanted to let the musicians take ownership of the songs.

I had scheduled a speaking engagement the following morning for an MS group in Pasadena, so we planned to meet in the afternoon at Station House Studio in Echo Park.

The first day of my session, I was nervous. Actually, I was scared to death, because I didn't know anyone except Shooter. True to his word, he had taken care of all the details, booking a studio as well as an engineer and musicians. Two of the guys had played for the Black Crowes, a rock group. Mark Rains, the sound engineer, ran the studio and lived in an apartment right behind the studio. "Ted" Russell Kamp was the bass player and bandleader, so he was the first to arrive. Ted was a touring artist who had worked in Nashville and referred to himself as "California country," so he was aware of my music. Jamie Douglass was the drummer. He and his wife were expecting a baby during the time we recorded.

Except for Mark, who looked like an insurance salesman, everyone in the band had long hair and beards and appeared as though they had walked off an album cover from the late 1960s or early '70s.

The studio itself was a vintage, quintessential 1970s rock-and-roll studio, with a large control room, a much larger open main studio with a grand piano, and a few small isolation booths for recording quiet instruments. One of the vocal booths had been an old meat locker in the market that once occupied the building. The walls were all covered with wood paneling, and I could only imagine the songs recorded and the stories those walls had witnessed. The studio lighting was a dim red tint.

Before I arrived, Shooter had told me, "I want to decorate the studio in Barbara Mandrell country décor, because I want a good vibe there. I'm gonna put candelabras everywhere."

I said, "Okay," and then went to google what a candelabra was.

Sure enough, when I walked in, Shooter had rented several large candelabras and positioned them on stands around the studio. Combined with the tinted red lights, the room took on a dark yet soothing and artsy air. Not since I'd worked with Brent Rowan had any other producer been so tuned in to me, going far beyond what was expected to make me feel comfortable and able to get mentally prepared to record.

We started with "Why Can't I Have You?" a song that Shooter planned to pitch to a Netflix show called *The Ranch*, starring Ashton Kutcher. I recorded the vocals as I always did, thinking of the lyrics. When I record, I close my eyes in the studio and snuggle up to the microphone as closely as possible. I'm a perfectionist and want the sound to be perfect.

To me, it seemed like a sad song. But Shooter saw it differently.

"Just be more playful with it," Shooter said. "Imagine yourself sitting by a swimming pool with a couple of your girlfriends, and you see a great-looking guy walk by, and you question, 'Why can't I have this guy?'"

I did, and the vocals took on an entirely different feel. Sure enough, it worked, and Netflix featured the song on Season 2 of the series. We were off to a great start.

I didn't know how Shooter's sessions worked. I didn't know what time we'd start, and I certainly wasn't accustomed to working all through the night. But that was normal for Shooter and his friends. The atmosphere was more like a party than work, because we were having fun.

We recorded until around two or three o'clock in the morning. Everyone was excited about what we had accomplished that day. I was exhausted, and then Kate and I had to drive to find a hotel room for the night. After that first session, I always brought a large cup of coffee or mint tea. I never knew how late we'd run, and I wanted to stay alert.

Before I arrived in California, Shooter had sent me another note. "I got a B side that I think you will love," Shooter wrote. It was "I Think You Know," a song that his mother, Jessi Colter, had written but had never recorded. It was an emotion-laden song about meeting someone new and almost instantly recognizing that there is something special about this person. I fell in love with the song, tucked it into my heart, and kept it as a special gift to me.

The second day I was in town, we recorded "I Think You Know." Although Shooter could play almost any instrument, including the piano, he brought in a keyboard player, Adam MacDougall, to play on the session. "I can't do it justice," Shooter said. He was proud of his mom's song, and I'm sure it must have been emotional for him. Shooter played the demo of the song on his phone, and Adam nailed it after hearing it only one time.

In a rather unique twist, Mark set up a microphone in the studio control room, rather than in the main room, for me to sing "scratch" vocals so the band could get the feel of the song as they played their parts. Singing in the control room lent itself to a warmer, more evocative feeling than singing in a vocal isolation booth.

To save money, Kate and I moved from one hotel room to another each night. I had shopped online and gotten the lowest rate, but that price was good for only one night each. So we moved every morning at checkout time and drove back to Echo Park each afternoon, which worked well because Shooter and the band never started working before three in the afternoon.

On one occasion, we had planned to start recording at

1:00 p.m. Kate and I arrived around 12:30. I knocked on the studio door but nobody answered. Finally, Mark staggered out in his sleepwear. "Did you not get the message that we are starting later than we had planned?" Mark asked through a yawn.

Kate and I went down the street to a coffee shop. Our one o'clock session started around four that day.

With the positive results of the first two songs fresh in our minds, Shooter and I started thinking about recording a full album. We recorded more than sixteen songs, far more than we needed for one album, but creativity was flowing, so we simply went with it. We even recorded one of my favorites, "Peace in the Valley," the song I used to sing for Carol, the young woman with MS who lived in the nursing home.

Shooter and I never had a conversation about money. For both of us, recording music was about creating art. Shooter produced the entire album at his own expense, pouring his time and talent into the project on the speculative hope of recouping his expenses and earning a financial return in the future, the very thing that nobody of his stature would do in Nashville.

I was accustomed to recording in three-hour sessions in Nashville studios, but Shooter didn't seem concerned about the clock. He was more interested in making art than he was keeping everything on time. He was totally laid-back, so much so that other than those first two songs, we never had a plan. We simply recorded what we were passionate about. "Let's just have fun," Shooter said. "Let's make a great record."

Every day was an adventure just walking into the studio. I showed up on a Monday, and Shooter was excited about a new song. "I went out to a show in Joshua Tree and heard this song called 'Big Moon,'" he said. He handed me a CD with the song on it. "I think you'll like it. Take this with you and learn it tonight, and we'll record the basic instrumental tracks tomorrow."

"Tomorrow?"

"Yeah, we'll work out the arrangement tomorrow and lay it down."

Once, I sent Shooter something that I had recorded by myself on my phone.

"I love that," he responded. "We'll record that tomorrow."

It was a totally spontaneous, fascinating way of making an album, and I loved it!

Shooter is a brilliant producer. He thinks things through in his own artistic way and sees the big picture, yet he allows everyone involved in the creative process the freedom of expression rarely experienced in studio sessions. "Let's just try it one time," was one of Shooter's frequent comments. Of course, we recorded several passes, sometimes into the wee hours of the morning, until everyone felt good about the results.

I stayed in California for less than a week, partially funded by the speaking engagement in Pasadena. It was the first of numerous trips I would make to work on the album. Because we had no advance money, I tried to arrange my speaking engagements around the times when Shooter was available to record. That way, I knew that the costs of my food and lodging would be covered by the group for whom I spoke. Rather than setting aside a few weeks to crunch out an entire album, we worked around Shooter's schedule and mine, matching availability with Mark and the band and recording when we had time—and when everybody felt like it!

It took us more than two years to complete the project, but we recorded some sensational music. One of the deeply personal songs to me was "The Song Goes with Me," which I wrote with Marcus Hummon after I had lost my record deal and left Mercury. In many ways, it is autobiographical, describing my relationship with music. I had felt so lost, and I wondered where I belonged. But I had realized that you can take my record deal away from me, but you cannot take the music out of my soul. I have the song within me, and it will go wherever I go.

As I closed my eyes and sang the song in the studio, I thought, *Everything can be taken from me, but music is deep in my soul. Music has always been with me from the time I was little and would sing songs along with Mama and my sisters in the white truck . . . to now, when it brought me to LA to make this record with Shooter.*

Looking back, I can see that everything happened for a reason—my troubled upbringing, my departure from Mercury, the movie being put on hold, my bad business deals, even the effects of the flood on my body—all forged my character and made me stronger. But sometimes it takes getting on the other side of the breakdown to see the beauty in it.

~~~~~

I still don't understand why some things happened, and occasionally, I ask God about that. But I know we aren't supposed to understand everything, so I just keep the faith and believe it all will make sense one day.

Before my trip to LA in March 2015, Shooter sent me a song, "The Concept of You," which he had received from his manager, Jon Hensley. He had originally intended the song to go to Wanda Jackson, but Jon felt it ought to go to me.

Shooter said, "Hey, I know this is really off the wall and not your style, but I think your sexy, lower range would be amazing on this tune. Maybe live with it for a few days. Imagine it being even more *Pulp Fiction*-ish . . . sultry and sixtiesish. It has a cool vibe. If not, no worries. But I thought you could nail it."

The style of the song was quite different for me and sounded as if it could be in a Quentin Tarantino movie. It was about a guy imagining a beautiful woman with whom he was in love but knew he could never be with. I could empathize with the guy wanting an amazing person in his life. I understood that need for love.

"This song may be really weird, but I think you could do it," Shooter said. "It's very theatrical, but I think we can make it you."

Unfortunately, Jon passed away unexpectedly during the recording process, and he never got to hear our version of the song he had suggested to us. Shooter flew to Kentucky for Jon's funeral, so I went with him to meet the writer, Michael Farmer, who also lived in Kentucky. After I met

Michael, I could better understand the heartache of the song, and I could wrap my head around the lyrics and make them mine.

"Music City's Killing Me" is a lament about the effects of the music industry on an aspiring artist. It was originally written as "New York City's Killing Me," by Ray LaMontagne. Shooter said, "I think you should do it. It is your story."

I recorded it as a duet with Jamey Johnson. He was on the RCA label earlier in his career and then moved to Universal. Jamey is a great country singer and has recorded a lot of songs, but he is not immersed in the business side of the music industry. He could relate to the lyrics of the song.

Shooter found a song titled "Devil's Pool," which his dad, Waylon Jennings, had started but had never completed. "Take this song and finish it," Shooter said to me. "My dad was writing this song before he died, but he only got as far as the chorus. I think you can write the verses. I've tried but I just can't do it. But I think you can."

Shooter sang the chorus for me, and I recorded it on my phone. "All I know about the song," he said, "is that my dad was around a lake or a body of water somewhere, and everyone told him, 'Don't swim in that lake because lots of people have drowned mysteriously there.' They went into the water and never came back out." Except for the chorus, Shooter had no lyrics for the song. He didn't even have a melody for the verses.

"Go back to the hotel and write it," Shooter said.

When I returned to the hotel, I called Mama. It was already late at night, and I felt panic creeping over me. "What am I gonna do, Mama? Of course, I'm honored, but I want to do this right. Shooter wants to record the song tomorrow, and I haven't even written it yet!"

Mama was calm as ever. "Julie, just go with the flow," she said.

"I'm trying, Mama!" I said.

That same night, while working in LA, I played a show with Shooter and his band at the Troubadour, a famous rock-and-roll club in Hollywood. We played some of my older songs and some of the new material we were working on in the studio. I had put out the word on social media that we were playing, so the fans started pouring in to the Troubadour, many of them wearing *Julie Roberts* T-shirts and paraphernalia. Before the show began, Misty said, "Julie, I think you have more people here than Shooter does. Look at everyone out there with your shirts on." I was surprised at the outpouring of fan support. I hadn't played on the West Coast in a long time, so the fact that so many fans hadn't forgotten me really buoyed my spirits.

It was a fabulous show, and it was extremely gracious of Shooter to share the stage with me. More than anything, I appreciated his confidence in me. I hadn't felt that from anyone in the music business in quite a while.

I went back to the studio the following day and said, "Shooter, I didn't get the words written, but this is what I think the melody for the verses should sound like."

"Okay, let's record it," Shooter said.

Record it? I barely knew how to hum it! But we recorded the melody to a song for which I had not yet written the lyrics. Then I just made up a story about the Devil's Pool. I didn't change Waylon's chorus, but I made it a story song, a metaphor like country music used to be, and I made it a warning to a guy not to date my sister. I finished the lyrics for the song, and we recorded it. We weren't sure what to do with it, but I was delighted to have had the chance to work on the song. And I had what few artists in country music history have ever had—a cowrite with Waylon Jennings!

Shooter had first contacted me by email in August 2014. We started recording in September 2014. We didn't work on the album every day. Far from it. We worked sporadically on the project, guided more by the content of the album than by a deadline or schedule. By late April 2017, the album was finally done.

Self-effacing as ever, Shooter said, "People are going to be shocked that you came out to LA and made a record with Dracula."

I had so much fun making this record. In the process, I had regained my confidence, and I felt this was my strongest album to date. Then came the difficult part—finding the right record company that would catch the vision for our artistic endeavor.

The frustration of having an album completely done and having to sit on it until the right opportunities opened became a lesson in patience for me. My idea of patience has always been reflected by that prayer, "Please, Lord, give me patience, and give it to me right now!"

But life doesn't work that way. And I know the music business doesn't either.

Nothing, however, is wasted in God's economy. He takes even what the enemy intends for evil, turns it around, and uses it for our good. I knew that he had brought me back into a reconciled relationship with Luke Lewis, and I was glad for that. He was now retired and was living in Charleston, South Carolina, so I called him and asked him if he'd be willing to meet with Shooter and me, and listen to our new album. I also knew that Luke might be able to help.

Shooter and I visited with Luke and played our music for him. He loved the new album, and he gave us three solid recommendations about who he felt would be receptive to the new sound.

I knew now that my life was not in Luke's hands, or Shooter's, or anyone else's. My life and my career were in God's hands. And as hard as it was for me, I knew I could not depend on people to open doors for me, but I had to believe in God's plan for my music and for my whole life.

23

Pig-Sitting for Lashes

As part of my new normal, I've had to be willing to do whatever it takes to maintain the type of top-quality show I want to deliver, even when it comes to my own personal appearance. Consequently, I've developed some expertise in an old-fashioned skill—bartering. For instance, I worked out a deal with Blush, a fantastic boutique clothing store in Nashville that provides me with gorgeous show clothes in exchange for advertising their store.

I have always enjoyed having my hair done and my eyelashes enhanced prior to doing a show. But having and maintaining eyelash extensions is expensive, and I couldn't rationalize spending that much money. But one day, Melissa Rhodes, one of the best eyelash stylists in Nashville, and I were talking about our love of animals. I told her that I have four dogs, and it is sometimes difficult to find someone willing to pet-sit them when I am on the road.

"Yes, I know what you mean," Melissa said. "I have a really difficult time getting someone to sit with my pig."

"You have a pet *pig?*" I asked. My mind saw a barter possibility. "Hey, I think we can do a deal here," I said. "It wouldn't be a stretch for me to pet-sit your pig in exchange for the beautiful eyelashes you create for me for my shows."

On one occasion while I was pig-sitting two-hundred-pound Lucy at Melissa's house, I was watching *Good Morning America* when I heard a knock at Melissa's front door. I didn't really want to answer it, since I was not in my own home, so I peeked out the window to see who was there. A woman holding a baby was standing on the front porch.

She might need help, I thought. *Maybe I better open the door.*

The moment I opened the door, the woman squealed at me, "Your pig's loose! It's way down the road."

My hands instinctively flew to my face. "It's not my pig!" I tried to explain, but that seemed irrelevant at the moment.

"My husband is chasing her already, trying to get her," the woman said. "He's had to get her before."

I ran outside and saw that people driving by were taking pictures of the man chasing the pig through the neighborhood. I later learned that they were posting pictures on Facebook and Instagram of the pig that I was supposed to be watching.

I'd felt Lucy's bite before, and although she was strong, I knew she wasn't ordinarily violent. But a bunch of kids were agitating the pig too. When we caught up with Lucy, the neighbor and I tried to tempt the pig with food to lure her back to Melissa's house. That didn't work. We tried to pull her back, but she ended up pulling the man and me down the street. We tried tempting Lucy with strawberries, Hansel and Gretel style, but the pig simply scarfed up the strawberries and didn't take a single step back toward home. We finally chased the pig into a neighbor's fenced-in back-yard. By now, Lucy was really angry and charging at anyone who dared get near to her.

Bystanders laughed as they called out to me, "Is that your pig?"

"No," I yelled back. "But she is my responsibility."

After several hours of trying to lure Lucy back to her own yard, the neighbor who was helping me said, "I have to go to work, but I have a dolly you can use. Put the pig's crate on the dolly, and leave strawberries in the crate. Hopefully, the pig will climb into the crate to get the strawberries, and you can trap her inside and roll her back home."

As outlandish as it sounded, his plan was my best option. I took his advice and after a while, Lucy fell for the ploy. She climbed into the crate to get the strawberries, and I quickly closed the lid and latched it.

I rolled her home and unlocked the crate. Lucy was exhausted. She crawled out of the crate, totally worn out, and spent the rest of the afternoon wallowing in the backyard.

I was exhausted, too, as I sat and stared at the pig. "What has my life come to?" I asked myself aloud. "I'm pig-sitting for lashes and then have to spend the morning chasing a pig through the neighborhood." I looked up toward the sky. "God, you sure have a sense of humor!"

While working with Shooter on the album, I struck a deal with a long-standing, reputable agency in Nashville to book my concert dates. The agency did their best, but booking an artist who was not on the radio charts and was without a new album was a difficult task. I understood and encouraged them to book every date possible, so they did.

No longer did I travel in a big, beautiful tour bus with my own bedroom in the back, but now I traveled to concert dates in a rented van, along with my band members and Mama when she could join us.

I didn't mind. I was willing to do whatever it took to reignite my career. Some of the places I played were a far cry from the enormous music festivals and other popular venues I played after my first record soared up the charts. In a few instances, I didn't even earn enough money to pay myself after paying my band members. But a gig was a gig, as far as I was concerned.

One particular place was a saloon-type atmosphere in a building that looked like a pole barn. I'd seen animals kept in better buildings. As my band and I pulled in, I was so aghast at the sight of the place, I had one of those breakdown moments and blurted, "Oh gosh, where are they booking us now?"

Immediately, I felt bad for saying it, as I am always

grateful for every booking, but some venues are definitely better than others. And this was one of the others. I turned and said to my musicians, "Hey, I'm sorry. Let's go do a great show, anyhow."

Interestingly, despite the fact that the showroom was terrible, the moment I stepped onstage to do a sound check, I was happy and contented. I was "home," doing what I love. The size of the crowd or the type of venue didn't matter. I thanked God for the privilege of being able to sing.

On the other hand, playing small, nondescript venues where a large percentage of the crowd is inebriated before I even begin my show can sometimes be dangerous. At a club in West Virginia known for its rowdy patrons, I was not scheduled to go onstage until after midnight. Several fights broke out before I went on, so I was already a little nervous as I started my show. All throughout my performance, a rough-looking woman stood in front of the stage, calling out to me, "Play 'Break Down Here'!"

"I'm gonna sing it for you," I responded to her. I normally performed that song late in my show, so I simply placated the woman and moved on.

"Play 'Break Down Here,'" she called again. "And dedicate it to me."

"Okay, I'll do that," I said to her from the stage.

We went through something similar after every song. I like to interact with my audiences, and I was having light-hearted fun with this woman. Strangely, just as I was about to do "Break Down Here," I saw one of the bouncers push to the front and escort the woman out of the club.

I later learned that she had already been kicked out of the

club earlier that evening for getting in a fight with another woman, and it had taken six bouncers to separate them and help them out of the club. She had returned to the club and asked if she could use the restroom.

The bouncer kindly allowed her back into the building so she could go to the bathroom. He escorted her to the restroom. Apparently, while the bouncer waited for her, she smeared her own excrement all over the restroom walls as an expression of her anger at being tossed from the club.

I was glad she liked my song, but I didn't want to mess with that woman! "There may have been some drugs involved in that situation," my guitar player quipped.

It is difficult for a woman to receive respect at some of those rowdy clubs. At a club in Mobile, Alabama, a deejay played loud dance music prior to my show. When it came time for me to perform, I waited offstage to be introduced, as I always did. The deejay also served as the emcee, so in an effort to hype the crowd, as he was announcing me, he yelled, "All right, y'all! Who all wants to get *laid* tonight? Okay! Here she is, Julie Roberts!"

That was not exactly the sort of introduction I had anticipated or appreciated.

When I returned to Nashville, I engaged in a serious conversation with my booking agent. "I don't think you are booking me in the right venues," I said. "I don't want to play any more places where I'm afraid somebody is going to get into a fight. If I'm not going on until midnight, half the audience is drunk in those places. I want to play venues where the audience can actually hear my lyrics and appreciate them as much as I do."

Sometime in 2015, Shooter and Misty moved to a new house in Hollywood Hills, and shortly after that, I received a message from a friend, saying, "Someone is writing horrible things about you on social media."

I checked it out, and sure enough, a Goth-looking woman, who was actually stalking Shooter, had posted vicious, vile messages that I was going to die like Sharon Tate, one of the victims who had been murdered by the Charles Manson gang in 1969. I had heard the gruesome story, but Manson had been in prison for my entire life, so I wasn't aware of the details. When I researched the murders, I was horrified!

I notified the police, but the authorities said, "There's nothing we can do until she actually commits a crime or does something illegal."

Thanks, that helped a lot.

Apparently, because I was recording with Shooter, and we were posting items on social media, the stalker decided that I had moved in on her "territory." Every time I posted something, she responded with obscene vitriol, and anybody on my social media outlets could see it. I talked with Misty and Shooter, and they, too, had received awful messages from the woman. Their only solution was to block the stalker from my social media. I did that, but it still scared me to think that there are people, who, for no apparent reason, want to hurt others.

I knew I had to take seriously the potential threat, because I had experienced something similar earlier in my career, when a stalker showed up first at my shows, and then at my house. He always wore black clothing and had dark, dyed-black hair that he wore in a mullet. He came to every show I performed anywhere nearby and many shows that were far from home. He showed up in the audience and always bought my music and photographs so he could stand in the merchandise line to meet me after the show and to have me autograph his purchases.

When I first encountered him, he had a young girl with him, and I noticed that she looked scared to death. At the time, I had no idea what sort of person was standing in front of me asking for an autograph. As I would do with anybody, I tried to be extra nice to him, but after a while, his unusual behavior became a matter of concern to Mama, my road manager, and even to me.

After each concert, when I signed albums and photographs, inevitably, the stalker purchased something and stood in line, watching me and waiting for me. Strangely, he demanded that I spell his name in different forms. He never wanted me to write his name in the same manner.

One time I posed for a picture with him after a show, and he squeezed me so tightly, I was afraid that he was not going to let go. I wriggled away from him and looked to my road manager. "Stay real close to me," I begged.

At first, when the stalker attended my shows, he stood off by himself observing me, but he was not rude or frightening. Then he started saying things such as, "I'm gonna take you away" and "Jesus made you for me." Once he told me, "We're going to live together forever in heaven." At other times, he threatened, "I'm going to take you with me, and I might let you call your mama."

The stalker typed out ominous notes inside greeting cards and either gave them to me at concerts or sent them to me in the mail. On one occasion, after I played a show in Nashville, I stayed late signing autographs and talking with people after the concert. Mama went home by herself, and she found a number of typed greeting cards on my car sitting in the driveway.

Mama called me and told me about the cards. "Don't come home," she said. "I don't know where he is, but he obviously knows where you live."

I called the police, but again there was little they could do. They took the cards to compare the handwriting with known criminals but came up with nothing. The stalker was a nuisance, but he had not committed any known crimes.

I was on tour in Europe when he showed up in Scotland at one of my shows. *Scotland!* He made a scene when I decided not to do a meet and greet before the show, as I usually did an hour before each evening concert.

The stalker got furious at my road manager and stormed away from the venue. I didn't see him in the audience that night—which was okay with me—nor did I see him afterward.

I did, however, see him back in Nashville. I was getting gas on the west side of town when I looked up and saw the stalker staring at me from across the parking lot. I hurriedly completed my purchase and drove away as quickly as possible.

I looked repeatedly in my mirror, watching for the stalker as I drove a convoluted, indirect route back to a friend's home in Nashville, rather than drive to my home. That was the last time I saw him, but I know he is still out there.

My experiences with him reminded me again why so many music artists and other celebrities pay so much for personal security.

I can't afford those high-dollar security companies, so I just pray a little extra for God to take care of me. And I'm so thankful that he does!

24

I Ain't Skeered I Have MS

I had called my music business Ain't Skeered Touring Company and later, Ain't Skeered Records. But it was a major turning point in my life when I was able to vocalize the words, "I ain't skeered I have MS!" Admitting my weakness forced me to rely more on God's strength, and it also helped me see myself and my purpose in a different way.

That began when Tony Conway introduced me to Jeannie Unruh, who became a significant part of my life by catching my passion to help others with MS. Jeannie had developed multiple sclerosis in her early thirties but was unaware that she carried the disease until after she was married and got pregnant. Researchers have discovered that MS often hides itself in a woman's body until she gives birth. Then like a wild animal released, the disease ravages the body. During pregnancy, Jeannie felt fantastic, but after giving birth to her first child, and the stress on her system, she manifested symptoms similar to mine—blurred vision, inability to walk, and being bedridden. It was only then that Jeannie's doctors discovered that she was living with MS.

She and her husband, Vic, began a vigorous regimen prescribed by her doctor to fight the disease in her body. Thanks to the program designed for her, Jeannie not only functions well, but she has had two more children. She and her husband have become tremendous advocates for helping others who are living with MS.

Jeannie and Vic host a fabulous fundraising event for the National MS Society called Crystal Boots & Silver Spurs, held annually on their property in Indiana. They had heard my music and a bit about my story, so they contacted Tony Conway about having my band and me play for their event and for me to tell my story. Jeannie and her husband flew in to Nashville to meet me and to learn more about how I was living with MS.

I knew I had met a kindred spirit the moment I laid eyes on Jeannie. By then, she had been dealing with MS for several decades, yet she was well dressed, her eyes sparkled vibrantly with an enthusiasm for life, and it was clear that she was a woman on a mission. That mission was to help other people who were living with MS. We connected immediately.

We talked about my music, the flood, and how I had first realized that I had MS. Jeannie shared her story with me and we compared notes. "What sort of therapy are you on?" Jeannie asked.

"Funny you should ask," I said. "I'm trying to decide what to try next. My doctor has given me about fourteen or fifteen different approaches, and I'm more confused than ever. I'm willing to do whatever is wisest and best, and I pray every day that the Lord will help me, but I just don't know what to do."

Jeannie and I talked at length about the various medical protocols available to people coping with MS, and she was actually more helpful to me than my neurologist. The doctor was excellent in providing clinical expertise, but in Jeannie I saw a woman who had been taking medications combined with diet and exercise for more than thirty years, and she was thriving. More than that, she was traveling the country and helping others!

Jeannie became a great friend and a mentor to me. I was not ready to join a support group locally, so having a mentor such as Jeannie was an invaluable resource for me.

At Jeannie and Vic's fundraising event, I met dozens of people who had passions similar to Jeannie's, some who had MS, others who were living with someone who had the disease, and still others who had a concern for funding research. It was tremendously encouraging to me to hear the stories of others living with MS and to realize that I was not in the battle alone.

At Jeannie's urging, I became more involved with the MS Society on a national level and on the local scene in Nashville. It was a turning point in my life when I accepted an invitation to stand in front of a group of people and speak about my experiences with MS. Like an alcoholic who acknowledges, "My name is Julie, and I am an alcoholic," I found incredible freedom in admitting to other people, "I am living with MS."

Through working with the National MS Society, I discovered a purpose I never knew I had, telling my story about living with MS. Prior to becoming a national spokesperson for MS, my prayer had always been, "God, please help me get back to where I want to be, singing music and helping to inspire people." I had no idea that God would answer that prayer in such an unusual way. It had taken me a long time to accept the fact that I had MS, but now I wanted to do everything I could to raise awareness about the disease.

When I was initially contacted by a local chapter of the MS Society to share my story, I was willing but reticent.

"What do I say?" I asked. "I don't know enough about drug protocols to speak authoritatively about what might be helpful to people."

"No, we wouldn't want you to do that, anyhow," the representative said. "Just tell people your story."

So that's what I do. I get to encourage people and tell them what I *wish* I had heard from someone when I was first diagnosed with MS. When I speak to others living with MS, I tell them, "Find those things that keep you going. For me, those things include my faith in Jesus Christ, my love of music, Mama, and my dogs."

Whether they are people of faith or not, they have to find something to live for. I know that everybody has to believe in something greater than himself or herself if he or she is going to overcome the prolonged fatigue that often accompanies MS.

I wanted to become more involved in the MS Society, so Mama and I participated in a fifty-mile walk in Charleston, South Carolina, to raise awareness and support for the organization's various programs—which are excellent and presented free of charge to those living with MS and their caretakers. It was inspiring to me just to walk along with other people dealing with MS, as well as caretakers and people from the medical profession. The Charleston walk was split into three segments over three days, so although it was a long-distance walk, it was fun. Some people walked the entire distance, while others walked only a mile or two, but all the participants were important to the cause of spreading the word that nobody has to live alone with MS.

I participated in another fifty-mile walk for MS in Savannah, Georgia, along with my friend Kate Marshall. On the Savannah walk, I met a young woman who had more than one member in her family coping with MS. She had enormous obstacles to overcome every day of her life, but with God's help, she was doing it.

It is sometimes awkward speaking to patients with MS. There I am standing onstage wearing a pretty dress and high heels, and the audience is dressed mostly in comfort clothes and many are seated in wheelchairs. "How can you walk in those heels?" an outspoken woman asked me in New York.

I smiled at her and told her, "I have my flip-flops right over there in my purse." I always do. "I wear heels onstage or for meetings, but I change into flats as soon as possible."

Sometimes I sense a disconnect at first, but I want to encourage others that they can live with MS. Often, the audience will listen politely but skeptically, until I touch on the one subject that seems to relate: my faith in God. It is my faith that brings significance and meaning to my life, more so than any accolades I have achieved.

"It might sound odd," I tell audiences, "but I am more fulfilled by having the opportunity to encourage you to keep following your dreams, despite the MS, than I ever was singing onstage to tens of thousands of people."

Travel is hard on me, and keeping up with my busy schedule sometimes wears me out, but I work hard to keep myself in good physical condition, and I listen to my body when I need some rest.

To help soothe my throat, I usually plop a Halls menthol throat lozenge in my mouth before speaking or singing. I opened one of the lozenges and discovered on the wrapper a positive, inspirational message: "Be unstoppable." I purchased more of that product, and I've gotten in the habit of reading one or two before every speech or show for my own personal pep talk. The lozenge wrappers have sayings such as, "Push on," "Power through," "Flex your 'can' muscles," and "Conquer today."

Recently I spoke in New York on the same program as a neurologist who really loved my story. He knew I was returning as a speaker the following year, so he asked one of his patients to come to hear me. This patient had tried to commit suicide twice because she was so depressed about having MS.

When I saw the doctor again, he told me that his patient

had listened to every word that I had said and had been encouraged that she could live a full life, despite the MS. As he told me about the young woman's response, tears streamed down his face. "She left so happy and positive after hearing your message," he said. "She's now facing every day with hope." He paused and said, "It's not because of me. It's because of you."

I went away amazed and thanking God that he could use me to help that young woman.

While I enjoy immensely the many events I attend as a spokesperson for the MS Society, speaking at their national programs and conferences, encouraging a large group of people living with MS, caregivers, and medical personnel, it is equally meaningful for me to speak to someone with MS one-on-one. These days, my ears are attuned to people needing help.

I was at a coffee shop one day in a business meeting regarding my own career when I overheard a conversation between two young women I guessed to be in their early twenties, sitting at the table next to me. I heard them talking about their friend who recently learned that she has MS. "She is so nervous," one woman said. "They did an MRI and found lesions. She is so scared and fatigued."

The hot-button words: *MS, lesions, MRI, fatigue,* and *scared* caught my attention. Before long, I found myself listening more to their conversation than my own. At first, I felt guilty for eavesdropping, and then I realized that I was supposed to be there.

Before the young women left, I stopped them and said, "I'm really sorry, but you caught my ear. I was listening to your conversation, and I heard you say you have a friend with MS who is nervous and afraid."

"Yes . . . ?"

"I'm Julie," I said, "and I've been living with MS for more than thirteen years now. I was afraid too. I speak for the MS Society, and I also sing for a living. I just want to give your friend my contact information, and if she ever wants to reach out to me, she can."

"Thank you so much," one of the young women said. "We'll tell her."

Several months went by before I found a message on my website from the young woman with MS. She told me that her friends had encouraged her to contact me. She was also in her early twenties, thinking her life was over because she had been diagnosed with MS. "I've been following you on social media, and you are an inspiration to me," she said.

I wrote back to her, "I'm so glad you contacted me. I was where you are thirteen years ago, so if you have any questions, I'm here to help. You can do this. Medications are readily available that can help you function normally, but don't delay. Get on that therapy regimen now. It will help slow the disease's progression."

I've discovered that I don't have to know all the answers about MS. Neurologists who have worked with MS patients for years are still stymied by some aspects of the disease. But I've found that I can be an encourager, offering people hope, letting them know that yes, we have a difficult challenge, but it is not insurmountable. Medical help is available; the

MS Society and other organizations offer incredible free programs providing information, practical help, and inspiration; and most of all, God's love and power are available to get us through.

~

As much as I try to live normally, I must keep in mind that a simple injury can be much more complicated for someone with MS. For instance, the day after the great pig escape, I was jogging downhill with my friend Teresa in a Nashville park when my foot caught on a skinny, hidden root sticking up in the path. I lost my balance and flew several feet through the air. Instinctively, I put out my hands to break the fall as I slammed awkwardly to the ground. I felt the pain mostly in my hands and arms, but I could tell that I had bruised my leg as well. I got up and brushed mud off my arms and legs and clothes. I started running again, but soon I felt my leg tightening. I stopped, and Teresa stopped with me. "Does my leg look normal to you?" I asked her.

"Oh no, it doesn't," Teresa said. "It looks like it is swelling."

I walked the remainder of the trail, assuming that the pain from the bruise would go away before long. But the following day, the pain was more intense, and the swelling was worse.

I went to the doctor and was grateful to find that I had not broken any bones. Unfortunately, the pain would not go away. It burned like a bad sunburn, and my leg remained grossly discolored. I went to work out, and while there, a woman approached me. "I noticed your leg, and it doesn't look good to me. Have you had that checked?"

"Yes, I have," I said. "Thanks, but the doctor said it is okay."

The woman shook her head. "I don't think so. I'd get another opinion."

I went back to the doctor, and she sent me to the emergency room to make sure that I was not developing a blood clot. At the ER, the doctor worried that I might have acute compartment syndrome as a result of a blunt force trauma. They videoed my leg and sent the clip to an orthopedic surgeon. "You may be having surgery tonight," the ER doc said.

This was not good. The doctors also put me on high dosages of steroids to reduce inflammation, a constant danger with MS.

When the orthopedic surgeon reviewed the case, he ordered that the fluid in my leg be drained immediately. I went home after the procedure, but the following day, the doctors changed their minds. "I think you should have surgery," the doctor said, "to reduce the risk of a blood clot."

"But I have a show this weekend."

My doctor didn't want me to go, but he knew I would. "Can you sit down onstage?" he asked.

"I could," I said, "but I probably won't."

The doctor sighed and smiled. "Okay, if there are no complications after the surgery, then you can go do your show, but please raise your leg above your heart as soon as you get offstage."

I had the surgery and was scheduled to perform the concert in Wynne, Arkansas, only one day later. My doctor reluctantly allowed me to go. My leg was bandaged, and my hands were still black and blue from the fall. Mama knew that I was hurting, so she suggested, "Julie, maybe you should cancel. You can hardly stand on your leg."

"Mama, I can't," I said. "The first time I cancel a show, people are going to say, 'She can't do it anymore because of the MS.' I have to go. I'll be careful, but I have to do the concert."

I went and played the show, and I was fine . . . until I came back.

On the way back, my fingers and toes and the palms of my hands turned dark blue. I returned to the hospital, where the doctor said, "This is the worst reaction I have ever seen."

The doctor admitted me to the hospital, worried because he could not explain what was happening in my body. More doctors examined me. They sent me to a blood specialist. The doctors still could not figure out why my body was turning blue, but they loaded my veins with steroids.

They sent me back to the doctor who had done the original surgery. "I think you have some sort of blood disorder," he said. "I want to check for everything. What you are experiencing is definitely not normal." He took eighteen tubes of blood from my body. He referred me to another doctor, who took even more blood. I was beginning to wonder if I had any blood left inside me!

It took more than a week to get the results. I waited and prayed—a lot.

When I returned to his office, I was worried, but the doctor seemed upbeat. "I want to run a few more tests, but your results all look normal. I didn't expect that." He took more of my blood and instructed me to return in two weeks. "We'll keep a watch on it."

Thank you, God, I prayed silently.

As we awaited further results, right before CMA week in June, I went to Atlanta to speak for an MS function. When I arrived at the airport, I realized that my flight was an hour earlier than I thought. I was really cutting my time close, and if I missed the flight, I would not make it in time for my speaking engagement. As I anxiously made my way through airport security, I placed my carry-on luggage on the conveyer belt and watched as it went through the scanners. I started to follow after it, when a security officer stopped me even though I was prechecked. The officer pointed at my legs. "We need to take off your bandages," he said.

"You what?" I had an open wound beneath the bandages. I certainly didn't want to risk infection by removing the bandages in a public place swarming with people. I protested, but the officer was insistent.

"Yes, ma'am. If you don't want to take them off, we'll have to search you."

I glanced at my watch. Time was running out. "Well, okay. If I have to. . . ." I hastily but carefully removed the bandages. The officer placed them on the conveyer belt and sent them through.

"It will be fine," he said, nodding toward my bandages as they went through the machine, "but I need to scan your hands." The officer stared intently at my blue hands. When he brought the security wand near my hands, a loud alarm immediately sounded. I'm not sure whose eyes were larger, the officer's or mine. "What is that alarm all about?" I asked.

The officer refused to tell me. "You'll have to come with me," he said, as he summoned two female officers. "We're going to take you to a private room to search you and all your belongings."

"What?" I wanted to show him my prescreened clearance again, but it clearly did not matter to this officer. He hustled me out of line and toward a side room. Once inside, the officers went through all my belongings and searched me, too . . . all of me. Meanwhile, I watched the minutes ticking away, worried that my flight was already boarding.

"I just had surgery," I said. "I need to get my bandages back on."

"Have you stayed in a hotel recently?" they asked.

"No," I said, "I was in the hospital."

The officers scanned my incision and finally said, "Okay, you are free to go." They cleared my bags and allowed me to reapply the bandages.

"Why did you scan my incision?" I asked.

"Well, believe it or not, some people actually attempt to hide drugs in an open wound."

I was shocked that he had suspected me, but I didn't have time to debate with him. I ran toward my gate and boarded my flight, just as the attendant was closing the door. I plopped down in my seat and breathed a sigh of relief.

The speaking engagement in Atlanta was especially meaningful, because I was able to encourage a number of young women living with MS. I was glad I hadn't missed out on that opportunity. Upon my return to Nashville, the doctors continued treating me with steroids, and eventually my skin color returned to normal.

The physicians were still baffled and never did figure out what was wrong with me. But the accident and subsequent complications reminded me that because I live with MS, simple things such as a fall along a running trail can affect me in ways that other people might not be impacted. That's okay. I've learned that when I fall, I can cry out for God's help. He lifts me up and gets me moving in the right direction again.

25

Stronger

Breakdowns still happen in my life, but now, rather than worrying or complaining, I've learned to look for the beauty in the breakdown. During the fall of 2017, I was performing some concerts with Shooter Jennings when our bus broke down in California. Worse yet, we were booked to play in Arizona the following day. We patched up the bus with duct tape and limped our way across the state all the way to Shooter's mom's home outside Phoenix.

We played a show in Phoenix that night, and then the next day I was relaxing by Jessi's pool, waiting for the bus to get repaired. I was listening to music on my headphones when I heard Jessi call my name.

"Julie, you are going to get sunburned out there," she

said. "Come inside so we can talk." I loved hearing Jessi's stories about Waylon, the music business, and most of all, her faith, so I was happy to comply.

What followed was an afternoon beyond anything I could have expected. We talked and talked and were having a grand "girls' time," so Jessi showed me her extensive collection of custom-made dresses. I hung on her every word as Jessi described each dress and where she had worn it, and even what shoes she had paired with each outfit.

"Go ahead, honey," she said. "Try some things on. We're about the same size." Jessi pulled out a green band jacket from her closet. "My friend who works for *Vogue* got this for me from Paris for my book tour," she explained. She handed the jacket to me. "This is your color green. Try it on."

I slipped on the jacket. "Oh, wow; I love it, Jessi! It's so cool and unique . . . and it's from Paris!"

Jessi walked all around me, gazing at my new look. "I'll loan it to you, Julie," Jessi said. "Keep it and wear it."

Our conversation drifted toward spiritual matters. Jessi shared some gospel songs she'd been working on, and she gave me a CD for those times "when you need some extra encouragement." We talked about one of her favorite Bible verses: "'For I the LORD will speak, and whatever word I speak will be performed. It will no longer be delayed, for in your days, O rebellious house, I will speak the word and perform it,' declares the Lord GOD" (Ezekiel 12:25 NASB).

That verse led to one of my favorite conversations I've had in my life. I confessed to Jessi that I sometimes felt ostracized because my music was not like most other artists', whose sound or material might be more commercial. "It's lonely being out here on my own," I admitted.

Jessi hugged me, and her words took on an almost prophetic tone. She suggested that, as her favorite verse implied, it would be only a matter of time before that promise of God would be fulfilled in my life. "Don't worry that your new album isn't like anyone else's," she said. "Things will work out. It just takes one person to hear you, but it needs to be the right person. God is bringing that person to you. Let's pray for that together."

Jessi prayed briefly, and then we talked further about our careers. "'I'm Not Lisa' was turned down by five labels," Jessi said, referring to her 1975 megahit song. "Like you, I was different," she said. "But different is good, and God made you different! That person is coming to your life who will believe in your music. You are special, and never forget it."

She sat down at the piano and sang two more spiritual songs for me. I cried as she sang. I was so thankful that our bus had broken down in Phoenix. Some days God sends "angels" to encourage us. He sent one to me in the form of a music icon.

That night, as I slipped into my bunk on our freshly repaired bus, heading to play a show in Tucson, I prayed silently, *Thank you, God, for this day and for the broken-down bus. I will wear Jessi's green jacket and remember every special word and the beauty I was given in the breakdown.*

A few weeks later, a friend invited me to a drop-in reception at her Music City office that had recently been remodeled, so I was happy to attend. The moment I walked in, a waiter greeted me at the door and offered me a glass of champagne. "No, thank you," I said. "It's water for me tonight." I was on a strict diet, getting ready for the photo shoot for the album I had done with Shooter. Although the album was not yet placed with a record company, I believed in my heart that I'd be doing photos for the album soon, and I wanted to look my best. I know that for me to feel good in my clothes, I have to cut out the mindless snacking (that I love to do) and track every healthy item I eat. So I passed by the champagne and fancy delicacies on the sweets tray.

Walking around the room, sipping my glass of water, I was stopped by a woman who seemed to know me. Although I recognized her, I could not recall where I'd met her. "Oh, honey," she said, "you and I worked out at the same gym ten years ago." We talked for a few minutes, and I thanked her for saying hello, with me wondering the whole time, *How in the world did she remember me?*

The woman then introduced me to her friend, a yoga teacher in town whose husband was in the music business. We recognized each other, and they both were wonderfully kind, expressing how much they loved my music.

The friend then spoke with sincere compassion, "Julie, it's great to see you, and I am so sorry."

"Sorry?" I asked, my face forming a quizzical expression.

"Yes," she said. "I heard the news that you were diagnosed with MS and could never sing again. It broke my heart for you."

My own heart seemed to stop for a beat or two, and I said, "Well, thank you, but I'm happy to tell you that the information you received is false. I have just finished record-ing the best album of my life!"

The friend was relieved. "I'm so glad that I was misinformed!"

I was thrilled to tell her my good news but also frus-trated. All I want is another chance to show the world that I can still sing.

Each day, I ask myself, *Am I doing enough? Did I email enough people to tell them that the album is done and will be available soon? Did I drive Shooter crazy, emailing him new ideas constantly?* I've always been a worker, and I want people to know that I am ready and willing to work hard to do what-ever God wants me to do.

I ask the Lord every day to give me some signs that I am on the right path, to show me the direction he wants me to go, and to give me just a nudge to keep going. Some days I see those signs, and on other days I don't. On those days when I feel as though I am floundering aimlessly, I'm sometimes tempted to become an Uber driver!

When I mentioned that to a friend, she said, "Really, Julie? You'd get lost in your house without a GPS." We both laughed hysterically.

But she wasn't done. "More importantly, do you really want to lose faith in God's plan and his timing in your life?"

"No, I don't," I said, "but I do need to pay my bills. I could wear a baseball cap and no one would ever know Julie Roberts, country singer, is also Julie Roberts, Uber driver."

"Well, two people would know that you were settling for something other than God's best for you," she said.

"Really? Who?"

"God and *you*," she said.

~

When you have a dream to do something great, every idle day feels like eternity. *God, did you forget about me? When is it all going to come together?* The toughest and sometimes loneliest room of all in God's house is the "waiting" room, waiting for the good things that you know he is going to bring to you and the good things that he is going to do in and through you.

Sometimes I get impatient and tend to worry. I know things take time, but the radio silence—when I'm not hearing my music on the radio—makes me so anxious. I've done my share of whining and complaining to God: *Lord, how long? Lord, when is it going to happen? When are things going to fall into place? How long must I endure?*

Usually the answer I've received from those prayers and laments of frustration has been, *Trust me, Julie. Don't put your faith in human beings, systems, companies, or even friends and family. Place your trust in me.* I'm learning that I can't really worry and fret and trust God at the same time. Worry is losing faith. And without faith in God, nothing good happens.

So I keep working hard and believing God for a great future. I refuse to allow myself to wallow in self-pity or to dwell on negative thoughts. Instead, I continue to dream, believing that God is going to do something even greater in my life than I've ever imagined. And this time, I have a different voice—one of strength, determination, and faith—one touched by the hand of almighty God, to be used for his glory and to encourage people.

So my prayer these days is this: *God, I'm available to you. Wherever you want me to go, whenever you want me to go, please open the doors. I'm ready and willing.*

That may not sound significant to some people, but believe me, it took me a long time to get to that point—a really long time. I used to look at all the magazines in the racks near the checkout lines in a grocery store, just to see if my picture was on one of the covers or if any of my friends were in the magazines. But for a long time, after I lost everything, I couldn't look at those magazines. Nor would I look at any of the billboards lining Broadway in Nashville, advertising some new music artist or event. And I'd quickly change the television channel or hit the Mute button if an advertisement for a music awards show came on the screen.

I was lost and envious. From the time I was a teenager, I had told Daddy and anyone else who asked, "I don't have a plan B. This is it." When people heard about some of the setbacks I've suffered, they sometimes thought they were being helpful and kind by saying, "But, Julie, there are probably all sorts of other things that you could do."

I appreciated their concern, and I always thanked them, but I never took their advice. I thought, *If you don't believe I can do it, then I am going to tune out what you are saying.*

When my first album came out, I experienced great success quickly and I tasted my dreams coming true. Maybe I took myself too seriously; I felt that I had to be perfect in everything I did and didn't allow myself to live in the moment enough. I was always looking for "what's next?"

Perhaps that's why God put me on pause. Looking back, I know I worried too much. I listened too much to the opinions of other people and their images of what I ought to be, rather than simply being myself. I even recorded a couple of songs that I did not enjoy singing—but someone else had told me, "Julie, this will be good for your career."

I went to extremes in diet and exercise programs, putting my body at jeopardy to be the size that "I was supposed to be" for photos or television. I wanted to please people rather than treating my body that God had made especially for me with care and respect and as the temple of his Holy Spirit.

Maybe God wanted to give me a few years to find that person who lost herself wanting to be someone else—to give me time to identify the things that make me the person who God created me to be.

I have to own the fact that I gave away my true self for a while, willing to do almost anything so I could live my dreams. Consequently, I didn't always show the world the person God made me to be, because I was so busy trying to please others and move ahead in my career.

When I was a girl, I loved to look into the windows of houses under construction, dreaming about the home I hoped to have someday. I wanted a house with more than one story, with ornate stairs, not merely a one-floor ranch style like ours. My best friend, Allison, who grew up in a loving, respectful family, had a big house with a great staircase, and I had promised Mama that I'd get her a house like that one day.

"Yes," Mama had agreed playfully, "and at Christmastime, we'll decorate it with garland on the banisters. I'll cook breakfast and you girls can all come down the staircase before we open presents."

For many years, that dream had motivated me. But I hadn't considered the ways the dream had made me selfish—that even though we had a perfectly comfortable townhouse with an attractive staircase, I was obsessed with buying a *bigger* house. How I desperately needed someone to look me in the eyes and say, "Get a grip, sister! You are blessed!" But I didn't realize it . . . until the flood came and swept our material possessions away.

I know God doesn't cause us harm, but I needed to be reminded what life is all about and what's important. And I got it.

I had to be broken in many ways, physically, emotionally, financially, and even spiritually, before I came to the point of realizing that I could either try to run my life, or I could trust God to run it. And although it might seem strange to think of it, I can almost imagine Jesus saying, "Okay, Julie, if you are going to break down, break down here. This is a safe place. I will protect you, care for you, heal you, and get you on the road—the right road—again."

Humility and brokenness . . . God has to get us there one way or another. And once we get there, we discover that we are not at the end of the world, but we are at the doorway to an entirely new way of living. Brokenness leads to blessing. God can take the broken pieces of our lives, and just as the Scripture teaches, he can make something beautiful out of them.

Since coming to that point of allowing God to pour beauty into my breakdown, I have a whole new perspective on life. Now when I go to the grocery store—guess what? I look at all the magazines near the checkout counter! Sometimes I even spend my hard-earned money on them so I can see what country music artists are featured inside, or what some person is wearing and what they do to stay healthy on the road. I'm not jealous; I am happy for my friends in the magazines.

And now when I drive down Broadway in downtown Nashville, I look up at the billboards . . . and perhaps, most difficult of all, I watch the award shows whenever they air. But instead of feeling envy, I picture myself in the audience, and I envision myself winning awards that we can put on Mama's mantel in our townhome. Well, we lost the mantel in the flood, but we can place those awards on the television cabinet that some kind person gave to us when we were trying to refurbish our home.

I'm still trying to figure this out, but I've grown so much in these past years. It hasn't been easy. I've been challenged in many areas of my life—my faith, my passion, my drive, my health, my happiness, my hopes—everything has been on a roller-coaster ride, with some bumps, twists, ups and downs, and sharp, unexpected turns. But my heart and my dreams have never changed. The little girl from South Carolina who wants to be a country music singer is still inside my five-foot-two-inch body. Nothing replaces the sense of fulfillment I receive from standing in front of an audience presenting a song or a special message. God put that desire within my heart when I was a little girl, and I believe it is there to stay.

But my motivation has changed. I no longer want to be a

star simply for the sake of being a success. I want to use the gifts and talents God has given me to help other people.

When I talk to young women nowadays, they seem intrigued by the obstacles I've had to overcome, as well as the good times I've enjoyed, so I am glad to share my stories with them. But I also gently warn them, "Don't do what I did. You are made in the image of God. Don't conform to what other people tell you that you have to be or think or sing or say. Be the beautiful person God created *you* to be. You will be happier and freer, and God will be pleased with you."

We all experience breakdowns in our lives in one way or another—emotional breakdowns, financial breakdowns, relationship breakdowns, and even spiritual breakdowns. But if we will choose to overcome, and if we allow God to use those difficult times in our lives, he will bring good out of whatever circumstances we face in our lives. Peace and contentment are possible as we see the beauty in the breakdown, to see that even in our broken places, God is still at work.

God never promises that we won't be discouraged, disappointed, hurt, or rejected. But he is right there with us. He never leaves us or forsakes us. That's why, when I've gotten knocked down, I've refused to stay down. I get back up and keep pressing forward. Resiliency and perseverance have been the keys to overcoming adversity in my life. And, of course, a never-give-up attitude and faith in God.

If we will trust him, we can find more than beauty; we can find God right there in the middle of our messes. He *does* bring beauty out of ashes . . . and sometimes, he even turns those ashes to gold!

Acknowledgments

I can't even imagine how this book would've happened without the love and support of so many people.

Mama, my other half, it is so hard to find a few sentences to tell you how much I love you. You saved me from a fire, from a flood, and from myself. You've shown me throughout my entire life what "ain't skeered" looks like! You continue to inspire me daily with your encouraging talks of faith and all your life wisdom. No matter how tough the times, your unwavering belief in my dreams is unmatched. I've laughed and cried more with you than with anyone on this earth. You always know how to find a way to make me smile through it all. You are the most beautiful, loving, and selfless woman I know. I thank God every single day he chose you to be my mama. I LOVE YOU!

Mawmaw, I'll always be your first "little darling" and carry that title proudly through my journey on this earth. Thank you for teaching me how to love and for always giving us a happy home when I was growing up. Thank you for all my singing outfits you made for me. You always knew how to make me feel special on stage!

Lorie and Marie, I love you both so very much! You lived this story alongside me, especially those early years. We always have been and always will be in this great journey together! Maybe one day we can have a "Roberts Sisters" reunion show!

Rhonda, Crystal, Philip, Jimmy, Shannon, Donny, Marissa, Luke, and Robby, I love you all! Thank you for your support and encouragement of my dreams all these years. There is never a substitute for family.

To my precious nieces, Torie, Emmie Grace, and Ashbie, I love y'all so very much. I pray you will always believe in yourselves and follow your dreams, forever. You girls can do anything you put your pretty little minds to!

Daddy, I want to thank you for my first real guitar and for my love of animals. I will always believe in you and love you.

Wren Franklin, this whole process started with you over lunch at Whole Foods. I told you that one day I wanted to tell my story in a book, and you so boldly reached out to two of the most amazing humans on this earth, Ken and Lisa Abraham. Without your initial belief in what I wanted to say to the world, I might not even be in this position of writing my acknowledgments. Thank you, sweet friend. I love you!

Ken and Lisa, thank you for believing I had a story to tell the world! You both have become my family. I will cherish every single hour I spent at your dining room table, talking to you about my life. You both have helped me get these stories out—the good and the bad—which is allowing me to move forward in a positive way. Thank you for all the laughs, the prayers, and even the tears you allowed me to shed in your home.

Lisa, not only did you cook so many delicious meals for Ken and me while we worked, but you have become one of my best friends. I am grateful for our long talks, all your advice, and our love of high heels!

Ken, you are like no other man I have met on this earth. You are not only a brilliant author, counselor, and friend, but you are a great husband to Lisa, a great father to your girls, and a great grandfather to your grandchildren. I started this process full of doubt that a man like you existed, and you showed me differently.

Which brings me to my next point: thank you, Ken and Lisa, for introducing me to my fiancé, Matt Baugher. I owe you for all the happiness this new chapter of my life is bringing me. We might even need to do a second book on this new journey! Are you in?

Ken, I believe, over tons of coffee, we have written a book of words guided by God. Thank you for bringing my story to life on the pages of this book. It's clear to me now why so many people call you the best in your field!

Matt, I had no clue when I was introduced to you by Ken and Lisa that I would be marrying you one day. God's plan is always so perfect, and I am so happy I canceled my event that day in April so I would meet you. You are the man I waited for my entire life, and I can't wait to see what God has in store for us. I always thought I would be the "Runaway Bride" until you asked me to marry you. For the first time in my life, I am not afraid of love, and I know for certain God orchestrated this long before we were both born. I love you, and I can't wait to do life with you!

Luke Lewis and Brent Rowan: Without the two of you, my music career may never have launched in the way that it did. It was fun reliving those memories in these pages. I'm forever indebted to you both.

Ron Shapiro, Tony Conway, and the other managers who've helped me along the way: I've learned something from each of you, and it has helped make me the best artist I can be.

To the amazing team at W Publishing and HarperCollins: Daisy, thank you for taking a chance on me! Megan and Meaghan, you made this book better on every page, and I've learned so much about book editing. Wow, what a process! Thank you, Kristen, for the wonderful packaging design! Denise, Kristi, and Becky, thank you for the marketing helps and for getting this story out there. I'm so impressed with your talents.

To all my friends: You are scattered across this great country of ours, and I wish I could say something about each of you, but I'm running out of room. I am blessed you are all in my life! Kate M.; Claire W.; Allison C.; Anita R.; Mary Margaret R.; Heidi F.; Mary Z.; Barry T.; Teresa M.; Renee S.; Renee A.; Erin M.; Kristen F.; Becky O.; Becky L.; Melissa R.; Marty V.; Jason C.; Linda S.; Ashley H.; Samantha M.; Danielle J.; Michelle P.; Kristi O.; Douglas B.; Adrienne H.; Alison S.; Amber W.; Daniel K.; Cory D.; Jessie R.; Janice M.; my hair gurus—Mark E., John F., Earl C.; vocal guru Rachel R.; Rebecca C.; Jeff S.; Stuart S.; Susanne P.; Patti B.; Lori B.; Rebecca J.; Molly K.; Danielle P.; Katie B.; Pat M.; Jeanie G.; Janelle K.; Stacy Mulder.; and everyone at the National MS

Society. I cannot name all those who have impacted my life, but you know who you are, and I love each of you dearly. Blush Boutiques, I love all the clothes you pick out for me—thank you!

Shooter Jennings, Misty Jennings, and Jessi Colter, I love you all so much. Shooter, you helped me find confidence in my own music again, and I cannot thank you enough. I love watching you perform and produce. I learn something new from you every single time I'm in the room with you. Jessi, I love your spirit so much! Your faith and positive spirit are gifts to the world, and I am blessed to know you. Thank you for loaning me your band jacket for a while. It will always be so very special to me.

To my mentor, Jeannie Unruh, and your wonderful husband, Vic: You have helped me in my journey of living with MS more than you could ever imagine. You are both heroes to me and so many living with MS.

They may not be able to read, but I'd be remiss if I didn't acknowledge my precious dogs and the joy that they bring to my life. Lucie, you are my guardian angel and have been with me through many of the chapters in this book. I don't know what I would do without your sweet face! Cosmo, you are the current man of the house and will always be my "first husband." Your "Jesus" eyes pulled me in when I rescued you in LA, and they pull me in every time we meet. Jessie, you are tough and survived the streets of Bakersfield for a couple of years, so you are a perfect fit in our family of survivors. Carlie, you are always hungry and the most vocal of all the babies—maybe because you've heard me singing in the house all these years. I love you all so much! Thanks for taking care of Mama when I'm gone on the road.

And to my Lord and Savior, Jesus Christ. In this life, we will always have breakdowns. But it is the presence of Christ that brings the beauty, meaning, and purpose to our journeys. I'm so thankful.

About the Authors

Julie Roberts stepped into the national spotlight in 2004 with her country music hit "Break Down Here." Her debut album earned RIAA gold for sales in excess of five hundred thousand copies. The South Carolina native was an undeniable sensation, performing in a wide range of concert and national TV appearances. Multiple honors followed, including an array of nominations from the Country Music Association, the Academy of Country Music, and the Country Music Television Awards.

In 2010, Julie took a hiatus from music to recharge her batteries and to confront a number of personal challenges, the loss of her home in the devastating Nashville flood, and being diagnosed with multiple sclerosis. Today, she is back, singing better than ever. She has returned to recording new albums and playing shows.

She is also a winsome inspirational speaker for the National Multiple Sclerosis Society and other groups, sharing how she lives with multiple sclerosis. "I want to inspire others to never give up on their dreams," she says. "I've asked God to use me to encourage others. I'll do that by continuing to share my story, recording new music, and playing shows. That's where my heart and soul are fulfilled."

Julie is also an animal lover, has four dogs, and is a strong supporter for animal rescue efforts.

⟶

Ken Abraham is a best-selling author, known for his collaborations with popular celebrities and fascinating, high-profile public figures such as former US attorney general John Ashcroft, senator Bob Dole, megachurch minister Joel Osteen, actor Chuck Norris, 9/11 widow Lisa Beamer, NFL football coach and NASCAR team owner Joe Gibbs, psychologist and founder of eHarmony.com Neil Clark Warren, former US senate majority leader Bill Frist, champion boxer and entrepreneur George Foreman, and ASCAP's gospel songwriter of the century Bill Gaither.

Fifteen books on which Ken has collaborated have appeared on *New York Times* bestsellers lists, with three of Ken's works reaching the number-one position.

Ken's recent bestsellers include *Walk to Beautiful*, with country music star Jimmy Wayne; *No Dream Is Too High*, with Apollo 11 astronaut Buzz Aldrin, and *More Than Rivals*, a gripping story of racial conflict and reconciliation, based on actual events.

At present, Ken has more than twelve million books in print.